Psychology Of Financial Success: Master Personal Finance

Book Option

Published by Book Option, 2024.

Table of Contents

Copyright

Published by Book Option

Illinois 40432 USA.

Copyright © 2024 Book Option

All rights reserved.

Thank you for having an authorised edition of this book and for complying with copyright law. No part of this book may be reproduced, stored in a retrieval system, or transmitted by any means, electronic, mechanical, photocopying, recording, or otherwise, without written permission from the copyright holder.

Psychology Of Financial Success: Master Personal Finance

Distributed by Book Option

For ordering information or special discounts for bulk purchases, please contact IngramSpark PO Box 14 Ingram Blvd, La Vergne, TN 37086 USA, 1-615-213-3525.

Design and composition by Book Option Cover design by Book Option For permission credits.

To offset the number of trees consumed in the printing of our books, Book Option donates a portion of the proceeds from each printing to the Arbor Day Foundation. Book Option has replaced over 500 trees since 2020.

First Edition

I dedicate this to the dreamers, healers, and givers who deliver value through art and invention, expression, and creation. With all my love.

About

Do you want to be financially successful? Are you tired of being in debt? Are you tired of not being able to afford the lifestyle you want to live? Well, if you are willing and ready to put in your time and effort into achieving real financial success then this Book is for you!

Most of my students are often surprised when I tell them that financial success is not about how much you earn. Pretty shocking right? After all, you would think that the more you earn, the more stuff you can afford and the better your life would be... Not exactly!

Your financial success and your success in general rarely depends on the amount of money that you are making. This, however, does not mean that we can be careless about the money that we make or that somehow money is not important. Personal finance is an extremely important aspect of our lives. If we are careless about our personal finances, we are also careless about all the other important areas of our lives, like our relationships, our careers, our education, etc.

Mastering your personal finances is a very important step that we all have to accomplish.

But what does success mean to you? To me, success means happiness, love, fulfilment, freedom and opportunities. And every single day I meet people who are not successful, whether they are wealthy businessmen or businesswomen, or fresh college grads who are barely making their ends meet. They are not successful because they have not mastered their personal finance. They are not successful because they did not yet understand success.

So, in this Book, I want to help you understand success. I want to help you master one very important aspect of our lives, our personal finance.

4

So, are you ready to take control of your life and your personal finance? Are you ready to start taking responsibility for your finances? Are you ready to finally start taking steps towards building wealth and achieving that financial freedom? Well, if you are ready, let's start this journey!

Introduction

This book has a strong emphasis on achieving financial success and the necessary steps to do so. No matter how much money we make, everyone puts in a lot of effort to earn it. We are tense all the time, and our concern never goes away. At the end of the month, we will consider all of our urgent expenses, including our rent, power bills, kids' school fees, premiums to be paid, and medical bills. Rather than enduring all of these hardships, what if we could create a financial strategy that makes our money work harder than we do, giving our children and ourselves a better tomorrow?

Reaching financial freedom is more than just having a high enough net worth or social standing. Furthermore, it is independent of your current income. The only thing to think about is how much of your income is being saved and how much is being prudently invested in a diverse portfolio. No other element can prevent you from retiring wealthy and early if you equip yourself with the fundamentals of financial freedom, such as the correct mindset and astute planning techniques. You may live your ambitions and achieve financial freedom by mastering the path outlined in this book. If you have made the effort to read this book and live the life of your dreams, I promise that if you put the tools, techniques, and strategies it contains to use, they will completely transform you and help you achieve financial freedom. It is true that "A journey of a thousand miles begins with a single step."

Recall that taking the first step is the hardest, but once we do, we may start racing in the direction of our destiny. If not, you ought to lead and manage your finances; if not, you ought to live a life of servitude. Make a decision for yourself; you always have the option to be the master or the slave of money. I have purposefully neglected all other factors in favour of the book's clarity and simplicity of style. This book is written in such a way that even a layperson may quickly read it and grasp it because of its extremely basic language. Recall that this book is not solely focused on perfection; you must acknowledge that mistakes are inevitable. As always, I suggest making a financial plan that accounts for uncertainties. Whenever you encounter difficulties, I rapidly make the required modifications to avoid a catastrophe. This book also aims to help you identify your precise desires so that you won't be seduced by your neighbour's brand-new automobile, glossy advertisements, or the newest technological innovations and end up spending your hard-earned money on the wrong things.

With the release of this book, I hope to provide you with an understanding of how actual financial planning operates and the fundamental stages involved in developing a customised plan that captures your own values and life objectives.

Reaching Financial Objectives

Discovering one's genuine life purpose is essential for leading a contented and prosperous existence. Every human being on the earth has a purpose, which they must discover utilising their individual gifts and abilities. Develop Gratitude: Upon awakening, express your gratitude to God for providing the necessities of existence, such as clothing, food, and shelter, for all of your possessions. Be thankful for every experience in life, good or bad, if you want to be content and happy all the time.

As a leader or team manager, you should always recognize and celebrate each individual's skills. This will motivate your team members to work harder and make you happier in the process. Use appreciation, the most powerful power you have, to transform your life. Clear thinking is the key to achieving any goal you set for yourself since everything in the universe is made of energy. You need to be very clear about your life goals, how you want your life to come to pass, and where you want to be in three or five years. You must take action in order to fulfil all of the above, and once you do, you can accomplish anything. Our subconscious mind guides us on our path once we have a clear idea of where we want to go; it functions as an internal GPS that will help us at all times. We should be able to think clearly in each of the following seven areas of life: career/business; how much money should I make? What is the appropriate profit target?

Number of Employees: Where should we focus our company efforts? Which kind of customers should be targeted? etc. Family Time/Recreation: Taking advantage of and spending time with family (parents, spouses, siblings, children, etc.); organising travel and tour plans; scheduling sporting events; etc. Individually defining your spiritual objectives and setting clear goals; taking up an activity you enjoy and changing it to see a new you; creating goals and making plans to reach them; etc.

Health and Exercise: Control your food, reduce fat intake, exercise daily, and meditate to enhance your inner self. Our physical appearance will also be improved. Financial investments in assets to develop wealth; net worth to be attained over time; income to be produced both actively and passively; house and automobile to enhance quality of life, etc. Setting SMART Goals in Life: Once you have clarity in your life, make sure your goals pass the following test: S-Specific (it should address the who, what, where, and when of the goal); M-Measurable (you should have milestones to track the progress of your SMART goals); A-Achievable (Ensure that the goal is realistic and not just a dream); R-Relevant (Verify that the goal is relevant to your life and whether it is worth your time to aspire to); T-Time-Bound (Deadline and timelines should be strictly adhered to). By taking the above steps, your goal should not only improve your life but also the lives of many people.

Finally, act; everything in life is achievable, and you will accomplish all of your objectives without thinking twice. Making a Goal Card: Write the following words on one side of the card: "Ask, and it shall be given to you. Search and you will discover. On the other hand, write your goal using the structure below: "I will consistently make it each month while leading a healthy, appreciative, and spiritual life. Knock, and it shall be opened to you." Steps to Reach Your Life and Business Goals: Step 1: Focussed Approach Having the following 4 increases the likelihood of taking a focused approach, which is my reality as of 2021. Goal Book: By writing down your objectives, desired outcomes, and the amount of time needed to reach them, a goal book helps you maintain focus.

Ideas Generator Book: Every morning, set aside at least 20 minutes to reflect on all the possibilities and ideas you had for where you wanted your life and business to be in three years. Bring forth fresh ideas to put into action to get you there. By going through this process, you will already be ahead of the competition. Make sure to record all of these ideas in an Idea Generator Book and continue to jot them down every day. Successful leaders and businessmen follow this, and there are many examples of people who have done so. Keep a gratitude journal and list all the people and things in your life that have raised your vibration on a daily basis. Make a Vision Board: Using a vision board clarifies your vision and helps you stay focused. Step 2: Subconscious Mind and connecting with the same As you may know, "A picture is worth a thousand words." This is one way to visually represent your goals, and as they say, "A picture is worth a thousand words." Let's get specific: Our mind operates in four key states: Alpha, which is the optimal state to program before going to sleep; Beta, which is the state we are in between awake and asleep; Theta, which is the state we are in while we are asleep; and Delta, which is unconscious and deep sleep state.

Additionally, studies have shown that meditation helps with mental programming. Step 3: Programming your mind and the two most crucial methods: Affirmations Affirmations are a tried-and-true method of achieving your goals, and they have the powerful ability to manifest as reality if you use them consistently. You may rewire your thinking by repeating affirmations on a daily basis. Positive affirmations for wealth and success include the following: I feel prosperous, successful, and happy; financial abundance is my birthright; I enjoy having a large wallet; I welcome financial freedom into my life; My inner child is deserving of financial success; I appreciate having wealth and abundance in my life; I allow myself to spend money on myself; I always think positively about money; and I am a conduit for innovative ideas for making money. Step 4: Divine

Planning By consistently utilising affirmations and visualisation techniques, your subconscious mind is able to receive all of your instructions. All of the opportunity, event, and concept planning and creation is done by the subconscious mind. It makes it possible for you to attract the correct people into your life in order to go toward your objectives.

It is no longer a coincidence that opportunities, ideas, people, and events find their way into your life; you have to be aware of them and be open to receiving them. Nevertheless, the programming in your head causes them to enter your life. Step 5: Finally, but just as importantly, be an Action Taker. Follow the instructions of your conscious and subconscious minds to carry out regular acts, no matter how big or small. "Always remember, action is the key to success." In some cases, if you are not seeing the intended outcomes, acquire input from mentors, dear coworkers, and others who are close to you. The secret to success is to "Never Give Up" on your objective; if you do, one day you will succeed.

Comprehending Credit Bureaus and Credit History

A Credit Report: What Is It? A credit report, created by a credit agency such as CIBIL (Credit Information agency of India Limited), is a comprehensive overview of a person's credit history. CRIF Highmark, Equifax, CIBIL, and EXPERIA are a few credit bureaus. Credit report types include Individual and Commercial. Detailed information on CIBIL score and how to raise it: A CIBIL score is a three-digit numerical summary of your credit history. It is calculated between 300 and 900 using information from your CIBIL Report's Enquiries and Accounts sections. A score that is nearer 900 indicates excellent credit, which increases the likelihood that the loan will be accepted.

According to the thumb rule, a credit score of 750 or more is considered good. Your credit score is largely influenced by the following factors: payment history and track record of the loan; defaulting on EMIs or dues; late payments are the primary factor affecting credit score and causing a sharp decline in the total score. Using Higher Credit Limits: Using higher credit limits and a higher current amount on your credit report suggest a heavier repayment load, which can have a detrimental effect on your credit score. The Credit Mix (Secured & Unsecured Loans): A balanced combination of secured loans (home loans, auto loans) and unsecured loans (credit cards, personal loans) is crucial. A balanced combination will significantly impact the CIBIL score overall. Multiple Enquiries: Every financial institution handling your loans must verify your CIBIL score if you have applied for more than one loan or credit card.

Receiving multiple credit card approvals or loans is a sign that your debt load has escalated. Lenders will evaluate your application cautiously, which will hurt you and lower your total score. Techniques for raising your CIBIL score: A strong credit history is a prerequisite for raising your CIBIL score, which is the primary factor that all lenders consider when granting a loan. First tip: Pay your bills on time by using an ECS or debit mandate. Lenders will take a bad view of all late payments, so make sure you pay the whole amount owed by the deadline. Hack 2: Low credit limit utilisation Reducing credit utilisation, exercising caution, and not utilising excessive credit all contribute to a higher credit score. Hack 3: Balanced Combination of Secured and Unsecured Loans: An excessive amount of unsecured loans may negatively impact your credit score and make lenders less favourable.

Make sure you have a good balance between unsecured loans (credit cards and personal loans) and secured loans (auto and home loans). Hack 4: Make informed decisions before applying for a new loan. It's crucial to apply for new loans cautiously because doing so won't show that you're asking for too much credit from lenders. Hack 5: Monthly monitoring of all Guarantee Loans, Joint Accounts, and Co-Signed Accounts: All outstanding balances from co-signed, guaranteed, and joint accounts are equally accountable for late or missed payments. Any carelessness on their part affects your future potential to obtain credit from lenders. Hack 6: Regularly checking Credit History Keep track of your credit history and check your score frequently to ensure that a lender won't deny you any loans that you apply for. How are you aware of your credit eligibility?

The ratio of allowed debt to income is 0.5. Let's look at an example to better understand: if Mr. X has a net income of Rs. 1,00,000 and total interest payments of Rs. 25,000, then his debt-burden ratio is 0.25. The likelihood of the loan being granted is increased but not guaranteed if the CIBIL score is above 750. Contesting the errors in your Credit Information Report (CIR): Accurate information will decrease the likelihood that your loan will be approved, thus it's equally crucial to fix all of the errors in your CIBIL report. Any changes require approval or authorization from the lender, which could be a bank or other financial institution, before CIBIL can directly approve them. The following are common mistakes: Incorrect personal information: If your lender (banks/financial institutions) receives inaccurate information about you, such as your name, address, date of birth, passport, etc., then CIBIL receives it as well. Any changes to a person's personal information, such as a wife's changed surname after marriage, should be reported to the appropriate banks or financial institutions so that their database is updated.

To guarantee the smooth application process for a loan in the future, any discrepancy in the information contained in the CIBIL report should be brought to the attention of the relevant Banks or Financial Institutions and fixed as soon as feasible. Mismatch in the overdue amount: If your CIBIL report shows a large overdue amount, it suggests you have additional debt to pay off and that you are not able to make your current loan payments. Lenders see these adversely, which lowers the likelihood that a loan will be approved. We must double-check with the bank or financial institution if the amount that is past due is greater than the actual amount; however, credit institutions often provide information on the final payment date of Dues/EMIs within 45 days. As a result, since the lender does not submit the data, the most recent payment might not appear in the CIBIL report. Ownership: These kinds of ownership adjustments should be contested right away through the Dispute Resolution Process (Total Turnaround Time is 30 Days) because there's a potential that other people's loans or credit cards may also show up in our CIBIL Report.

Using a credit card improperly is as simple as using it to make purchases you don't need to make with cash you don't have. This is one way that credit cards are misused. In modern India, carrying a credit card in your wallet is considered a status and luxury item. Before you apply for a credit card, ask yourself the following questions: What credit card debt do I currently have that I cannot afford to pay off right now? Are you saying that using a credit card won't immediately affect my bank balance and that you don't have to pay it now? Credit cards are appropriate only for people who are responsible enough to avoid going over budget. A credit card should not be a part of one's wallet in order to live a better, simpler life. It also brings great comfort to know that there are no credit card payments to pay at the start of each month.

Making Sensible Decisions Early In Life

Time is the most important factor in investing, and the earlier we start, the better. The biggest fallacy in investing is that it takes a lot of money to make a lot of money. Research indicates that early attainment of financial freedom is a result of starting early, and that the most important success factor is time. It is important to keep in mind that timing is not as important in the market as time, and there is no better moment to get started than right now. Therefore, don't waste time worrying about being early or late; instead, act quickly and get started. Start early since, as was already mentioned, time is of the essence. In order to comprehend financial freedom and help investing become a way of life, I would advise everyone to start investing as early as possible, even with pocket money, and to teach their children about investing as well.

My primary ambition when I started my work in banking in 2010 at the age of 21 was to settle down. However, at that age, advice on how to construct a route and achieve financial freedom would be a blessing if you were lucky enough to receive it. Take Mr. X as an example. He has a son who is ten years old and a daughter who is twelve years old. Mr. X has opened savings accounts for both of them, and they know exactly how much of each child's monthly pocket money should go toward savings and investments. Mr. X's son and daughter would gain a great deal by understanding compound interest concepts at a young age. There is a greater likelihood of reaching financial freedom sooner. The lessons that Mr. X is teaching the children are not ones that they would learn at school. Therefore, parents should start teaching their children about finances at a young age and cover the fundamentals of the topic openly. When we make an effort to improve by 1% each day, life tends to get better and everything around us gets better.

Allow me to go over some key takeaways from the book The Richest Man in Babylon. Regardless of how comfy your current employment is, set away Rs. 10 each month from your salary for every Rs. 100 that you earn. This amount will compound over time and eventually provide you an everlasting sense of contentment. For whatever reason, you do not need to be in this scenario if you are unable to save even 10% of your income. Believe me, it makes little difference if you are making 100% of your income or 90% of it after your 10% savings. Ideally, as soon as you are paid, put 10% of your take-home pay into an investment account and use the rest for either wants or bills.

Understanding Compound Interest, the Eighth marvel of the World: According to Albert Einstein, "Compound Interest" is the eighth marvel of the world. Those who grasp it rcap benefits, while those who ignore it incur costs. By definition, compounding entails generating interest. You must start early to have the "unfair" advantage over those who start later and comprehend the basic concepts of money if you want to compound, which will unleash its power over time. The best strategy is to "start early" in order to avoid the compounding effect. What is Warren Buffett's secret that enabled him to amass a billion-dollar empire? Investing for a long period, choosing the proper firms, having some lucky genes, and the compound interest effect have all contributed to his fortune. The investment amount of Rs. 12,000 at a cumulative interest rate of 10% annually for a 25-year horizon is shown in the above table.

We get another corpus of Rs. 13000 (more than the invested amount) as interest in the eighth year by investing just Rs. 12000 in the first year. With time, the compounding impact starts to work. The power of compounding comes into play when it comes to the next principal amount, which took only 3 years to reach the invested amount after it took 8 years for the interest to reach the invested amount in the first place. Long-term rewards come from being patient and giving it time: success does not come easily, and you can also benefit from compounding's magical effects over extended periods of time. You should be aware that the final 20% of your investment tenure, which is intended to help you attain financial freedom, accounts for more than 80% of your corpus. Recall that you should begin investing as soon as possible and not put off making purchases. We must learn to live with delayed gratification, and the invested quantity ought to remain in our investment nest egg for a longer period of time.

Achieve Peak Performance By Comprehending Investments

Everyone aspired to become an investor, trade in the stock market, and make an investment in a firm. A Demat and trading account is required. Let's first examine stockbroking companies, their functions, and the variety of broking firms that exist before delving deeper into the world of stock markets. Greetings, fellow investors! Learning how to invest is a popular topic, and everyone is eager to do so. Let's first discuss stockbroking firms, their functions, and the variety of broking firms that exist in India before getting into the topic at hand. Stock Broker: Rather than its clients, a registered member of the stock exchange, whether an individual or an organisation, is granted a licence to engage in the securities market. They take direct part in the stock market on behalf of their clients, charging a commission for their services.

It is our duty as investors to be aware of the costs we incur for commissions, annual maintenance charges (AMC), account opening charges (AOC), and trade-related fees. Prior to that, we must comprehend that stockbrokers in India can be classified into two categories. Full-Service Brokers: Kotak Security, Sharekhan, Motilal Oswal, HDFC Sec, ICICI Direct, etc. are examples of Traditional Brokers. Discount Brokers: Upstox, Zerodha, ProStocks, RKSV, Trade Smart Online, SAS Online, etc.; sometimes known as Budget Brokers; my personal experience: I began investing in 2009 with ICICI Direct (Full-Service Broker). I quickly saw that it was excessively costly compared to the other cheap brokers and never used their research recommendations or advising services. I came to the conclusion that it was pointless to pay ICICI Direct additional brokerage fees because I was not utilising their advising service. I switched to Upstox (Discount Broker) after that.

The prices were significantly lower than what I had anticipated; there are no AOC (Account Opening prices), no equity distribution fees, and very little AMC. Which broker—discount or full-service—should you pick? You will need to make the final decision based on the answers provided above. If you currently have a demat account with a full-service broker (ICICI Direct, HDFC Sec, SBI Demat account) and you trade infrequently and would like to save annual maintenance fees, I recommend that you convert to a basic services demat account (BSDA). The advantages of this type of account are shown in the table below, which varies depending on the stockbroker. An Initial Public Offer, or IPO, is what? a privately held business that is permitted to trade on stock exchanges such as the BSE and NSE and offers shares to the general public. The company's ability to raise funds more readily is the main advantage of going public.

The money received can then be put toward marketing, R&D, growth, and expansion—or whatever else a business needs to get off the ground and turn a profit. The internet application process has made it simpler to apply for an initial public offering these days. Typical Grievances of Investors Following IPO allocation: How come some people receive an IPO allocation while I never do? Is there something I'm not doing right? How can I improve my chances of being allocated to an IPO? How do I obtain an IPO Allotment confirmation? Why do IPOs have excessive demand? Good IPOs are oversubscribing with a very strong volume in the retail area. You have very little probability of receiving an allocation for a single application. You can apply in an IPO from the accounts of several family members to get around this. Apply a single lot to the Retail Category accounts of several family members. Compared to the case of a single application of five lots, the likelihood of a successful allocation increases to five times.

Additionally, you can open a HUF account, but to do so, you must apply for a PAN card under the HUF category in addition to opening a new Demat, trading, and bank account. You can submit up to five IPO applications from a single bank account with a select few institutions, such as SBI, Union Bank, and Axis Bank ASBA process. Let's compare the Listing Day Gains for a few firms in 2020 with IPO Subscriptions. Source: www.chittorgarh.com Capital raised in FY 2020 through IPOs: Rs. 31,000 crores was raised in total through 16 companies in 2020 through IPOs. Average Returns to Investors Who Got Allotment for the IPO's in FY 2020: Source: www.moneycontrol.com Average Returns to Investors Who Got Allotment for the IPO's in FY 2019: Source: www.moneycontrol.com

Conclusion: Carefully consider the following factors before investing in any company through the IPO mode: The company's fundamentals, financial strength, industry prospects, and any other significant facts and figures.

These Eight Rings Will Get You Into The Exclusive Financial Empowerment Club

There is no quick route to success; instead, a careful plan and set of procedures must be followed in order to achieve financial empowerment, which in turn leads to financial freedom. We achieve the true benefit of steady income throughout life without putting in long hours at work by adhering to a realistic and doable strategy, and we achieve Financial Freedom in the truest sense. It doesn't matter how well you live; if you don't have several sources of income, you will never be financially free.

By adhering to the eight rings listed below, anyone may learn how to create cash without putting in long hours at the office. The wealthy and those who love what they do do not have a retiring age, according to recent surveys and research. Your major objective should be to get wealthy sooner rather than later and to work in a sector you enjoy and that keeps you motivated every day from the moment you wake up until you are ninety-nine. We become obese when we spend our entire day in one position and accomplish nothing; the same is true with money. You won't see any growth at all if you keep all of your money hanging around. Rather, in order to begin increasing your money, you must make it work or exercise it. Your goal should be to grow your little nest egg into a sizable sum of money so you can live your life as you like and become financially independent as soon as possible. Make sure your money is invested wisely, and financial freedom will come naturally. By the time you've reached this chapter in the book, you must be really committed to your early retirement and financial empowerment.

I advise you to enter the Financial Empowerment club with the eight rings, and make sure you adhere to this plan religiously. The Eight Simple Rings to Financial Empowerment are as follows: Ring 1: An Overview of Cash Flow Planning; Ring 2: Know your Net Worth as of Today; Ring 3: Understanding Protection; Ring 4: The Secret of Buying or Renting a House, That No One is Talking About; Ring 5: Develop a Financial Freedom Plan; Ring 6: Diversification is the key to achieving Financial Freedom; Ring 7: Systems Pass, People Fail; Ring 8: Start celebrating with your family members for every milestone you achieve. Let's first review the eight rings and make plans for your entry into the Financial Empowerment Club.

Ring 1: An Overview of Cash Flow Planning: Even though you are doing a good job and earning a respectable monthly, you should also keep an eye on your spending. The following are some questions you should be asking yourself: How much did it cost you to live last month? When you add up all of your sources of income, how much did you make last month? Thus, cash flow planning takes into account both income and expenses. Finding out exactly where your money will be spent (both on needs and wants) and where you currently stand in terms of controlling your cash flow should be your first steps in the analysis process. Regardless of income, 95% of people are unable to reach financial freedom, and improper cash flow management is the primary cause.

Monitoring monthly income and expenses may seem easier, but often the most effective things are also the most overlooked. Since you work more than 36 hours a week to make a living, you should examine your past three months' worth of spending to see exactly where your money is going. All I'm asking is that you set aside two to three hours to break free from your more extravagant spending habits and return to the real world. Act immediately; keep in mind that an arborist will spend eighty percent of his time honing his axe.

If you want to do anything amazing in life—something that only 5 percent of people worldwide can accomplish—you have to think outside the box, which is extremely challenging and requires making many sacrifices. Let's look at all of your income sources: monthly income after taxes, bonuses, rental income, business income, pension income, investment income, and any gift income from parents or relatives.

Now let's look at your outflows of cash: how many rentals are you paying if you live in a rented home? Outflow for annual maintenance charges? What is the total cost of your children's education, including the annual fees and transportation costs? What is the total amount of premiums you pay for health, life, house, and auto insurance? What are the bills you are paying for water and electricity? - What is the cost of your family's and your own medical checkups? What is the monthly amount you spend on clothing for yourself and your family? What is the amount of donations made to nonprofit organisations? Daily expense tracking has excellent results and can cut costs by up to 20%, according to a recent research. Together with my spouse, I keep daily tabs on all of my spending, and she owns the ledger, which she updates each month. Like other habits, keeping an expense log of this kind should become second nature. Over time, the findings will surprise you.

Your total monthly savings potential, or the difference between your monthly income and spending, becomes known to you once you have finished the entire procedure. It could be challenging at first, and it can take you a month or two to fully grasp this activity. Ring 2-Net Worth Analysis: As you advance in life and work, the majority of you are primarily concerned with your current situation and your income, whether it comes from a paycheck or a business. Now is the perfect time to work on your study of net worth, since it is the only indicator that can help you get closer to financial freedom.

The difference between your entire assets and total liabilities is your net worth, by definition. Total Liabilities: Total Value of everything you owe Total Assets: Total Value of everything you own When your assets continue to increase in value above your out-of-pocket expenses, you are getting closer to achieving financial freedom without having to continuously add more money to your assets. You won't have to worry for the rest of your life if inflation is taken into account and asset returns are higher. Since you don't obtain an asset's market value during the liquidation process, assets are typically valued cautiously. Just keep in mind all of your possessions that you are unable to sell right away, such as your car, sofa, refrigerator, house, etc. Additionally, since you have the opportunity to liquidate at any moment, the investments you made for the second house and other properties can be regarded as assets. Recall to take into account the assets that, at some point in your life, you may be able to liquidate in order to support your expenses or generate higher returns by deploying elsewhere. of course, this should be your final choice.

Your monthly credit card payments, the interest you pay on your home loan, the cost of your insurance premiums, and other out-of-pocket expenses are examples of liabilities. A quick overview of all the debts includes outstanding credit card debt, which has a high default interest rate, outstanding home loans, outstanding auto loans, outstanding school loans, insurance premiums, and any other debt. Lastly, you must compute your net worth by subtracting your liabilities from your assets. Finding the ultimate sum marks the beginning of your path to financial empowerment. This is what makes you unique, and in order to make a name for yourself, you must increase it to the point where you can become financially independent and take an early retirement. Ring 3: Comprehending Self- and Family-Protection In this section of the book, we talk about protecting ourselves and our families. Protection is of two categories viz.

Individual health and life insurance policies. The sole purpose of insurance is to safeguard the family in unpredictable circumstances without jeopardising long-term financial savings, although these days, everyone purchases insurance for completely unjustified reasons. For a little minute, close your eyes and picture yourself not being there. When the family's primary provider is absent, it is a significant loss. The family will be severely financially burdened following the emotional trauma. What if you had to pay back your house, your car, and your debts? Your life resources should not be spent on your children's overseas education or marriage in order to pay for the EMIs; instead, they should be put to good use. In my personal life, I witnessed a family's entire unit crumble after the death of their kid. My very best friend Srinivas passed away from a heart attack at the age of 28 when I was doing my MBA. Everything was fine up until that point. Then, one day, we had a presentation to give, and none of us could find him.

A few hours later, we discovered he was dead. We all had a terrible day, and when I met his parents, I learned of their true financial situation. My friend did not have life insurance at that point either. Though his loss to the family is irreplaceable, his family would have had more financial security if he had taken out a life insurance policy. You should have understood by now that it's perfect for taking out a sizable life insurance policy. Calculating the total sum assured for all of your policies and the amount of life insurance your family will receive in your absence is one urgent chore you should accomplish right now. Term Insurance: The only product that should come to mind when we talk about life insurance is term insurance, where your premium is the amount you pay to obtain a life insurance policy. Let's use the following scenario: you are a 26-year-old paying an annual premium of Rs. 10,000 for a one crore rupee life insurance policy. This is the price you pay the insurance company for taking on the risk of your premature death.

You receive nothing back if you live past the policy's term and take out this policy for 40 years. Since the premiums you have paid are not being refunded, many of you think it is a waste of money. In this case, I strongly advise you to reconsider your own beliefs. It is the lowest cost you will ever pay for a life insurance policy, so you should wish that you pass away at a young age and that your family won't receive the one crore insurance life insured sum. We must comprehend the workings of endowment, moneyback, and unit linked insurance plans (ULIPs), which are the other market policies. Typical endowment insurance includes life insurance, which typically provides a life cover equal to your premium payment ten times over. For instance, if you pay Rs. 1,00,000 in premiums annually, your life cover is Rs. 10,000,000. It guarantees a return in addition to the life insurance, giving you a safety net for your family. In addition, a return that is tax-free at maturity and the annual premium you pay are covered by the Section 80 (C) exemption from taxes.

This is where you should look over your yearly results. If someone is able to watch markets but lacks experience in finance, their only option for investing in other asset classes should be an insurance policy for life insurance. Understanding Rule 72: Applying the Rule of 72 to determine your annual rate of return and the point at which your money doubles is a simple method to comprehend the dynamics of enormous numbers. You must calculate how many years your money will double and then divide that figure by 72. For instance, if you invest Rs. 5,00,000 and it doubles to Rs. 10,00,000 in 15 years, you will receive 4.8 percent a year if you divide 72 by 15. Therefore, it is best to avoid combining insurance and investments; instead, get a pure term insurance policy that pays ten times your yearly salary and keep your investment portfolio apart.

For example, if you pay an annual premium of Rs. 1,00,000 for an endowment program, roughly Rs. 3,000 will go toward your life insurance, based on your age and the amount you have left in investments. To attain financial freedom, it is therefore best to invest the remaining cash in wealth-creating items (stocks, mutual funds, etc.). Having ten times your yearly income or twenty times your monthly expenses is the recommended amount for life insurance. Let's use an example to talk about this. Assume you make Rs. 10,000,000 a year. If so, your life insurance should be at least one crore rupees. If the worst happens and your wife and kids inherit one crore without any financial education, she can, at most, use the money to open a fixed deposit. They can live comfortably for the duration of her life and earn about 6% interest annually.

Additionally, make sure you add life insurance to all of the larger loans you take out in your lifetime, such as the 80 lakhs home loan, so that your death won't be an immediate burden on your family. After taking out the loan, purchase an equivalent term insurance policy; never take out a decreasing cover policy, the premium for which is bundled with your home loan EMI, as these policies are more expensive, and your annual income will increase as you age. In a similar vein, your life insurance should rise as well. The optimum time to purchase life insurance is when you first begin working, when age is on your side and the cost of the premium will also be lower. You are the one who has to take care of your parents, thus the optimum time to supplement is when you have dependents, such as after you get married and have a dependent spouse and children. Importance of having medical insurance In addition to having life insurance, one should have adequate health insurance for themselves, their spouses, their children, and their dependent parents.

One should also avoid being in a scenario where they discover they have the incorrect policy after they are admitted to the hospital.

Therefore, having medical insurance is crucial to your quest for financial literacy. In my opinion, having a good, comprehensive medical plan is more important than having life insurance because the likelihood of being hospitalised for an illness is higher than the likelihood of dying. Rather than using up all of your savings to pay for hospital stays, it is preferable to have comprehensive medical coverage for the whole family, including parental insurance. For example, I recently visited with a friend from school, and after talking with him about how long it had been, I discovered that the majority of his life earnings had been used to pay for a recent health issue that his father had experienced. My friend thought that his employer would pay for it. Upon arriving at the hospital, he discovered that parents were not included in the group insurance and that the company's medical coverage was limited to the nuclear family. Thus, I would advise everyone to have separate health insurance from their job as most insurance plans will only pay for pre-existing conditions and their associated medical expenses for a maximum of four years. Consider a scenario in which kidney stones are discovered, you receive treatment, and after six months, you require surgery.

It's best to enrol in the second health insurance as soon as feasible because your medical plan won't pay for the procedure. We will be able to attain our financial goal of Financial Freedom at a younger age and prevent a decrease in our savings in this way. Prior to finalising the medical policy, make sure you fully comprehend the following features and pay the premium: Make sure you fully comprehend the NCB (No-Claim Bonus); thoroughly review the pre-existing diseases clause; ascertain the exact amount that the policy will cover for pre- and post-hospitalization costs; and identify the medical policy's exclusions. The policy or agreement you are entering with the general insurance company should not contain a co-pay clause.

Examine the disease waiting period clause. Look for sub-limits. Get the detailed list of daycare procedures where we are not required to stay in a hospital for more than a day. Understand Critical Care Illness (CCI) Cover: Critical illnesses are more common in the current generation. Diseases like cancer where you may not spend more time in the hospital like 24 hours hospitalisation. Nevertheless, you wind up having to pay hefty fees out of pocket. Chemotherapy takes three to four hours to treat cancer, yet the cost for a single session might reach lakhs. These serious illnesses will also significantly impair your ability to work; you will become less productive quickly, which could have an emotional and financial toll on you. In conclusion, everyone should get critical illness insurance, which pays out a sizable quantity of money as soon as the disease covered by the contract is diagnosed. About thirty-one significant illnesses, including cancer, stroke, severe burns, renal failure, organ transplant, heart attack, and end-stage liver and lung disorders, are covered by the bulk of the policies. Therefore, the best Book of action when selecting a life insurance policy is to include critical illness as a rider and select a plan where your premium is constant throughout the duration of the policy.

Ideally, a CCI policy should cover roughly two to four years' worth of your annual salary. Everyone should have critical care illness insurance, regardless of age, and the age range where this is most common today is between 35 and 45. This incidence age is decreasing as time goes on because of difficulties with lifestyle and climate change. These days, heart-related diseases affect males more frequently than cancer-related diseases affect women, and both are common critical care illnesses. Benefits of a Critical Illness Cover: This lump sum payment, which may be temporary or permanent, helps you make up for lost income from losing your work. gives you the choice to relax at home. offers you the choice to receive treatment. Reasons for the increasing trend in critical illness include:

sedentary lifestyles; irregular or insufficient exercise; processed foods high in residual chemicals; and unhealthy habits like alcoholism and smoking.

Ring 4: The Secret of Buying or Renting a House, That No One Is Talking About: Everyone wants to own a home, but before assuming that it will be a profitable long-term investment, it's advisable to conduct some research. By delving deeper into this subject, we may comprehend the majority's difficulty and one of the most difficult decisions of their lives—renting or purchasing a home. The cost of residential real estate is typically skyrocketing in metro areas, which has led many people to choose to rent rather than own.

Among Indians, it is well noted that those who can afford to buy a home tend to do so rather than rent, and for the others, it is never easy to determine what is best for them. Why do most individuals own a home? pride in obtaining a sense of security and becoming a homeowner. It's an enforced savings plan for a newly employed person's loan down payment. Individuals frequently believe that making EMI payments results in receiving two benefits: a month's worth of housing and a rise in the percentage of the house that they own. Rent, on the other hand, is only a monthly payment that doesn't result in the creation of any tangible property. Investing in real estate, which is also a real asset, yields tax benefits and capital appreciation. Being a homeowner instils a great sense of emotional pride in oneself. Why do individuals typically favour rental homes?

In metropolitan areas, paying rent is typically not more taxing than paying EMIs, which are typically nearly 2.5 times costlier. The added cost of home tax and other various fees is another drawback of property ownership. One should rent a house closer to work or the kids' school if the purchased home is far from either, even though the rent for such property could be out of their price range. A substantial amount of money does not have to be paid out in full up front for a down payment; instead, it can be saved for future investments that will eventually yield larger returns. Thorough examination with a computation example: Deciding whether to buy or rent a home has proven to be a difficult decision. In order to make an informed choice, let's examine the following two scenarios: Scenario 1: Purchasing a Home Assume Ms. Ramya has purchased a home worth Rs. 60 lakhs, with a 20% down payment of Rs. 12 lakhs, a bank loan of Rs. 48 lakhs at an 8% interest rate, and a 20-year loan period. assuming she is in the 30% tax bracket. Next, after taking into account the applicable tax benefit, we compute the effective interest rate payable and determine the effective monthly instalment that must be paid.

We arrive at total maintenance for the full 20-year period together with the net outflow as interest paid after taking into account the maintenance cost and the general growing trend of about 5% in maintenance. The difference between the appreciated property's worth and the whole cost of purchasing the property—which comes to Rs. 1.74 crores—is the net benefit of purchasing the property. Scenario 2: Hiring a Residence Let's say that Ms.

Ramya has made the decision to rent a property rather than buy one. The monthly cost is Rs. 15, 000, and there is an HRA advantage at the 30% tax band in addition to an 8% general rental rise. The difference of total savings for the period and total rent paid for the period, or Rs. 2.0 Crores, represents the net advantage of renting a home. Conclusion: Aside from all the computations mentioned above, there are a plethora of other aspects that must be considered when deciding whether to buy or rent a home. These elements include emotional and financial ones.

Ring 5: Create a Financial Freedom Plan: Just as we need to set goals for our lives, we also need to have a well-defined financial plan. As the saying goes, half the battle is won when you have a solid plan. You will discover a variety of creative ideas and wealth-generating chances along the way to financial freedom as you go on your money box trip and begin working on these plans and aiming to accomplish within the allotted time frame. Make sure you understand the following ideas, create a simplified financial freedom plan, and take the lead on your financial journey. Examine your current financial situation, group all of your investments into good and bad categories, and then dispose of all of the investments in the bad category.

Determine your net worth using the information from Ring 2. The precise quantity of money you needed to reach financial independence should be stated. Spread out your assets over the best asset classes, and monitor the expansion of your portfolio. Before beginning the financial freedom plan, make sure you have all the numbers in mind. If not, make a note of these details in an excel sheet and write down your final target amount, your desired age to achieve financial freedom, your monthly expenses, and the fact that inflation is one factor that continuously depreciates your money. Plan your investment vehicles so that they outpace the rate of inflation at any stage of your investment journey. Here are a few financial planning pointers: There are no shortcuts in life, and taking financial ones could end up short-circuiting your investment journey; make sure you have a sizable emergency fund and critical illness insurance; start saving for retirement as soon as possible; and make plans for special occasions like your children's marriage and education. Ring 6: The secret to achieving financial freedom is diversification.

Choosing the appropriate investing tool for each asset class in line with your long-term objectives is just as important as creating your financial plan, which is only the first step. Let's now examine a few financial instruments: Fixed Deposits and Recurring Deposits: Most of you are probably familiar with fixed deposits, which offer higher interest rates than savings accounts. Put a small percentage of your portfolio into fixed deposits because the principal amount is guaranteed and the interest rate is known. In the event that you are an experienced investor with exposure to various asset classes, make sure it does not represent more than 10% of your portfolio. Mutual Funds: If you have never invested in stocks before and are just beginning your path towards capital markets, mutual funds are a great place to start. As they say, "Always remember that Time in the Market is more important than Timing the Market." Your prospects of reaching financial freedom are higher the earlier you begin your investing path. A Systematic Investment Plan (SIP) can be initiated with a fixed monthly commitment for a predetermined duration.

Ascertain that you adhere to the following: Maintain everything online; these services are currently offered by a number of platforms; link your mutual fund account to your active bank account. As the initial step toward beginning your mutual fund investing adventure, it allows you to finish your KYC (Know Your Customer) online. Within a year of beginning your career, start your systematic investment plan (SIP). With time and a few market cycles under your belt, you will be able to choose better mutual funds as time goes on and your market knowledge grows. Buying mutual funds straight from the fund house, where you receive the fund at Direct NAV (Net Asset Value), is recommended because buying through a broking firm entails paying higher AMCs (Annual Maintenance Charges).

Consequently, this will yield a higher return on investment over an extended period (every penny saved is a cent earned) in the stock market: Jim Rogers once said, "The way to be a successful investor is to do nothing until you know it is going to work and is backed by your research." Once you comprehend mutual funds, you will know that a fund manager oversees a collection of companies and, upon deduction of fund management charges, distributes the returns to investors. The next step for you is to go into the stock market, which is the long-term most profitable financial instrument. I see a lot of people who are afraid of the stock market, but the people who are prepared to study and put those lessons into practice are the ones that get financial freedom more quickly. Let's start with a few fundamental stock market tips. Make sure the investment you are making won't cause your cash to erode, and never invest just on suggestions or ideas.

Instead, conduct due diligence before making a decision. Invest in large cap corporations and blue-chip companies early on, when there is less risk of capital erosion because they are well-established businesses with strong financials. The stock market is not the right location for you if your investing horizon is less than three years. You should be ready for both the highs and lows of the market cycle because stock markets are very volatile. A few excellent places to start are www.nseindia.com, www.bseindia.com, and www.valueresearchonline.com. You should always invest in companies that will provide you with both capital growth and consistent cash flow in the form of dividends. Never forget that stocks are best used as a long-term investment instrument since they provide the benefits of compound interest and rupee cost averaging, which work over an extended period of time. Gold: If achieving financial freedom is your goal, you should think about investing in gold through government-backed gold bonds or exchange-traded funds (ETFs). Everybody has interacted with real gold at some point in their lives. It is acceptable to hold physical gold up to a maximum of 10% of the portfolio.

Eventually, as it entails renting lockers from the bank for safekeeping, it will become a burden. Let's start with a few fundamental gold tips. As said in the previous point, register a Demat account, buy government-backed gold bonds or gold ETFs, and start investing with as little as one or two units. Gradually increase the units in ETFs at every dip to avoid owning actual gold beyond a certain point. Keep your gold investments invested since they serve as a portfolio buffer against inflation. Add gold to your portfolio with every 10% decline in price, and you can be confident that over time, the returns will be at least as high as the rate of inflation. One should keep a careful eye on gold prices, as they typically move in opposition to the general economic outlook and stock market values, in order to fully appreciate the importance of diversification.

Investments in gold had double-digit returns whereas stock markets have provided a single-digit return over the same period at different market cycles. Ring 7: People Fail, Systems Pass Becoming wealthy does not happen in a flash or in a single instant. Every transaction has a carefully considered pre-plan. It was the result of years of zeal and hard effort. Take the example of a football player's contract; it is the outcome of years of consistent practice, learning all the subtleties of the trade, giving up all leisure activities, and investing significant time every day in a never-ending process. It's not always a sign of a one-day success when we read in the media about some young guy who made millions of dollars through a brand-new online business. It's the outcome of a lengthy process in which he gave up a lot of significant things in order to accomplish his objective. Those who still hope for quick success and a major discovery should give up on their prayers and focus on the procedures and frameworks. Wishing for a single large, quick win will lead you to make bad choices, such as playing the lotto and investing in unknown, dangerous ventures. It takes time and a lot of hard work and effort to establish a self-sustaining system or product that will allow you to reach bountiful prosperity and eliminate the need for work. Even when you're not working and are asleep, it still makes money.

For example, J.K. Rowling's best-selling book series, the Harry Potter Books, has brought her enormous success over years of hard labour and effort. She amassed a multimillionaire fortune thanks to the sales of her novels. The best method to get rich quickly is to develop a system or product that will allow you to make money whenever you want. To do this, you must first identify a market gap, then draft a strong business plan, and finally acquire all the skills required to put the system into action and improve both society and your own situation. Despite what you have been taught since you were a child, you do not need to limit your thinking to that of a consumer with a never-ending demand for goods. Instead, begin to train your mind to think like a producer. When you encounter an advertisement in the media, for example, you automatically interpret it as if it were directed for the consumer, and you end up focusing on the product. You concentrate on how to obtain it and the joy it will provide. You keep yourself from seeing past the marketing by adopting this mentality. Consider a product from the producer's perspective to gain further insight into its marketing approach and product design.

Subsequently, you will disclose the characteristics that contribute to a product's success as well as the approach you need to take to market it. Additionally, to have a deeper understanding of a company's business tactics, find out how a product is made, where it is often manufactured, and how it makes money by looking at its revenue model. You should be aware by now that the old-fashioned get-rich schemes are no longer viable if you want to live your life as you choose, attain financial independence, and launch your own company offering a good or service. Ring 8: Begin sharing your accomplishments with your family. Your entire path to financial empowerment and financial freedom requires a great deal of work and effort on your part as well as that of your loved ones. Remember to be grateful for all the sacrifices made by your family members.

Whether or not your savings are going according to plan, once you have a clear objective and target amount of money, everything will fall into place eventually. This is independent of your current salary level. Make sure your family members understand the significance of each Financial Step and continue to celebrate the accomplishments with them in order to make them feel even more unique and include them in our financial journey. Nothing can stop you from achieving financial freedom for you and your family as long as you have a clear route and goals for how to get there. When discussing money problems with family members, try to keep things simple because they may find financial jargon and terms confusing. You and your family should concentrate on periodically honing your financial saw in order to reach financial freedom.

After you understand the rules of the game, make sure you keep beating inflation by learning the appropriate information and making the appropriate investments in financial assets. Synopsis of all 8 Rings: We want answers to every question we have regarding money because we live in a world where there are interest rates, credit cards, stock markets, commodities, and a lot of figures to deal with. Make sure that everything in your life is abundant, since money will always be there to support us. The money or riches we create will be there for future generations, despite having the ability to endure beyond our deaths. Make sure everyone you love who is dependent on you has received the attention they need. The appropriate asset classes are used with your money to provide higher returns. This book explains how to follow all the rules to build large fortunes and attract prosperity from the cosmos. In order to ensure that you are happy in this life, try to use the limited money and resources you have to give back to society.

A small number of extremely wealthy people who never give anything back to the community will never be able to change, and they will never be able to achieve financial independence. Additionally, keep in mind that money is not the only factor in success and that this book alone won't make you wealthy or financially independent. You can achieve financial freedom and an early retirement by investing in yourself and adhering to sound financial rules. These are the sole factors influencing your growth.

A Metamorphic Voyage From The Commonplace To The Exceptional

We are conditioned from an early age to live prosperous lives. We must do our best in school, work hard, land a decent career, accumulate money, retire, and then live off of our savings for the rest of our days. What if you could change your life from ordinary to spectacular by adopting the proper perspective and approaching riches in a novel way—something that isn't taught in schools or universities? It will result in a wealthy retirement, early financial independence, and a fulfilling life filled with no regrets. The Secrets to Success with the Wrong Mindset Uncovered: Everyone believes that luck or fate holds the key to wealth, and those who hold this kind of thinking are not wealthy and are risking their chances of success and a prosperous life.

A well-crafted plan is all you need to take charge of your destiny. Anyone who makes appropriate financial arrangements, such as setting up a life insurance policy, health insurance policy, and investments that provide compound returns over an extended period of time, is protected from unexpected financial setbacks like job loss or illness. Spending habits should also be controlled because, in the event that you become unemployed and live paycheck to paycheck, you won't have enough money to cover your monthly expenses. Even with an excellent wage, having a mindset that does not accept responsibility for your life in such a situation will not keep you going very long and will ultimately drive you to bankruptcy. We've all heard tales of individuals who won large sums of money from lotteries or big hits but quickly lost everything because they didn't have the right attitude. Your 9 to 5 job is not enough to retire wealthy and youthful. From an early age, our minds are constantly working through various strategies, such as obtaining a good education, which leads to a well-paying job; working even harder and accepting promotions to earn raises in pay and better opportunities for grades; and finally, when you reach the age of 50 or 60, retiring and living comfortably.

However, the catch to this strategy is that you cannot become wealthy by relying solely on your income. Furthermore, we must keep in mind that you have set working hours and that they are not endless. You will never be able to enjoy wealth accumulation when you reach old age since your body cannot support it when your joints hurt. Therefore, it is best to retire early and enjoy all the benefits of having good health and vigour, which will complement your hard work and help you lead a happy and tranquil life.

Never forget that while having money can make you wealthier, having money does not make you wealthier. Real wealth is the sum of things that make you happy and fulfilled. It consists of three primary parts, and we need all three to be happy. Our physical well-being and general health rank top, followed by independence in second place and meaningful relationships in third. Having a lot of money won't make you wealthy, and nobody will consider someone who is miserable and lonely to be affluent. All in all, this is done to get financial independence and freedom. It is advisable to amass riches; for example, once you have enough to live comfortably, you won't need to exchange your time for money, as you currently do in your employment.

Consequently, as you amass wealth, you will eventually get the liberty to allocate your time as you see fit, travel to destinations that pique your curiosity, and engage in any activity that brings you joy. Reaching financial independence entails living where you choose, pursuing your interests to the fullest, and taking as many expensive trips as you wish. Recognize that while money has a limited and finite impact, possessing a lot of it makes you wealthier. Avoid investment myths at all times, and pursue lifelong learning. Earl Nightingale, "The Strangest Secret in the World" Setting and achieving a goal motivates you to perform at your highest level, work with others, wake up in the morning, and take any necessary action. More than sixty years ago, Mr. Earl Nightingale, the owner of an insurance agency, made the decision to videotape a lecture intended to inspire his sales force. His success speech has grown so much that it has made him well-known, sold over a million copies, and earned him the first Spoken Word Gold Record.

Key Takeaways from The World's Strangest Secret: In this golden age of abundant options that we currently live in, people don't think or act the same way. His recording begins with the premise that, among 100 persons starting at age 25, every single one of them has faith in their ability to succeed and live happy, fulfilling lives. However, only one will be wealthy by the time they are 65, four will become financially independent, 41 will still be employed, and 54 will be impoverished and reliant on others for their basic needs. What Success Means Achievement is the steady accomplishment of a noble goal. You must be aware of your objectives, the reason behind your everyday job, the project you are working on, the motivation behind you, and the noble ideal. According to Earl Nightingale, nine times out of ten individuals don't know why they wake up in the morning. To which one might respond, "Well, everyone wakes up in the morning to go to work, so we also wake up." Establishing Goals Is Essential. Setting objectives is like a ship sailing out of the harbour, according to Earl Nightingale. Because the ship has a clear objective, a captain and his crew who have plotted the route will, for the most part, arrive at their target.

On the other hand, the crew and captain won't know where the ship is headed if the route isn't planned out. The ship goes nowhere as soon as it leaves the harbour. "All you need to get to your destination is the courage to push through with the plan and the road map." — Nightingale, Earl. To compete, all you have to do is produce. All you have to do to break free from the 9 to 5 grind and attain financial freedom in life is create a new product or service that solves a problem, using the wealth of resources available to you, such as open-source software, various articles, prototyping techniques, and free YouTube tutorials. The results are superior and there is a far larger probability of growing the prospects, despite the fact that it requires a significant investment of time and energy. How to Become What You Think About: The Secret Being aware of the ideas you are allowing to enter your head is one of the largest issues facing the modern generation. I can attest from personal experience that this definitely works.

Every person who consciously considers a goal from the moment they wake up until they go to bed will make daily decisions in their life that move them closer to their objectives. You will be able to reach your goal with clarity in this wonderful procedure. Establish the seed in your mind's subconscious. Our mentality is so intricate that it determines our level of happiness and achievement; many wealthy individuals nevertheless feel unfulfilled and unworthy of praise in their life. Never forget that success comes before money—the opposite is not true. Set daily intentions in your subconscious and keep repeating them so that one day they will come true. The Insider Secret on Five Crucial Life Principles Revealed Use your creativity to reach your objectives. What you think today determines who you become. You ought to have the bravery to focus on your objectives every day. Set aside 10% of each dollar you make. We must act as though ideas have no value unless we implement them. The fact is that everything in life that is free is valuable. Many people take for granted things like their mind, body, and health, which are non-replaceable and arrive with no strings attached. On the other hand, although expensive items may be replaced quickly, they are prioritised over other things that are necessary to succeed.

Achievement is never free, but it is simpler to achieve success and wealth if we are willing to put in the necessary effort, dedication, and hard work up front. Six Guidelines regarding Concepts have little value unless we put them into practice. Everyone has a ton of ideas, but ideas alone won't make us wealthy; we must put them into practice. It may be a million-dollar idea, but it won't work until and until we take action. Since its publication, millions of people have benefited from this audio version, which has also aided the personal development sector. We must fully embrace Earl Nightingale's advice in order to accomplish our goals more quickly and easily. You should be imaginative, create goals, maintain a happy attitude at all times, and make sure you are action-oriented. The following Six Crucial Principles are: Give yourself a clear objective. Go back to your early years and consider the reasons you believe you are incapable of succeeding. Instead of focusing on all the reasons you can't succeed, consider all the reasons you can Give up putting yourself last. Write a description of the kind of person you would like to be in order to alter the way you see yourself. Play the part of the prosperous person you've chosen to be.

Putting Procedures In Place And Making Connections To Make Money Work For You

After going over every financial notion, we must realise that the best investment is to organise your funds so that you can go forward in life without hassles or concerns. Rather than creating a one-time fix for every issue or challenge we encounter along the way with our finances, we ought to develop a system. All of the money you have made while working has been used to pay for a variety of bills, including living expenses, rent, Equated Monthly Instalments (EMI), child care costs, insurance premiums, taxes, family vacations, and a long list of other expenses.

Create a Cash Flow System to Improve Cash Management: Even if you have plenty of experiences to share, the majority of you avoid talking about money with friends and family because you think it's uninteresting. Many of you lament that you have no idea where your money is going; you only know when it first appears in your bank account; after that, it vanishes really quickly. You should be concerned if you find yourself in a scenario where you are unable to keep track of the money that is coming in and going out. In situations like this, individuals say the following: 1. I have no knowledge of how my money is spent; 2. I have no money left over to save; and 3. I have never considered investing since I lack the funds. You must have a strong cash flow structure in place to stop all of the aforementioned issues. Using a cash flow strategy entails setting financial boundaries between spending and saving. You may have a system in place, but it's only in its basic form and hasn't been properly defined. It's not necessary to have every app on the market to keep track of your spending—that can be challenging to achieve.

Long-term management is difficult, and on top of that, you are unwittingly giving away all of your personal information and spending patterns to a third party. The whole process is completed if you adhere to a basic cash flow system. To keep the savings account and the spending account apart is the aim of this approach in the money game. When there is a lot of money in the bank account, it is quickly spent impulsively and disappears from the account. Frequently, we use the leftover cash for unnecessary purchases or give a sizable sum of money to a buddy in non-emergency situations. They won't spend the money you lent them correctly after a while, and your prospects of getting it back are slim to none. Beyond financial gain, your friend's positive relationship will be irreversibly damaged in that scenario and gone forever.

Using the three buckets for the three purposes of money is an efficient approach to use the cash flow system: Income - Payroll Account; Expenditure - Payroll Account Investing and Savings Account All three of these categories benefit from naming. Divide the pay into three equal parts as soon as it is received: 20% should go into the savings account, 30% should go into the wants spending account, and 50% should go into the needs spending account. The more money you can put aside for savings, the easier and better it will be for you to become financially independent. An income account is more than just a record of your pay. It should include every type of income you receive, such as monetary presents from loved ones, bonuses from insurance plans or investments, rent from the house you own, profits from mutual funds or stocks, repayment of loans, etc.

Your spending account ought to now be divided into two: 1. Expenditure Account for Desires 2. Using the Needs Spending Account. This area includes all of your necessities, such as housing, utilities, healthcare, transportation, insurance premium payments, food and grocery expenses, rental costs, kid fees, and any other unavoidable expenses. They may account for up to 50% of your earnings. Any expenditure that is not urgent but yet desirable falls into the want category. Examples include shopping for luxury goods, holidays, the newest technology, and food and clothing beyond necessities. These expenses can account for as much as 30% of your income. Make sure that over 20% of your income is allocated to an investment account. Start with 20% at first, and make sure the amount rises to motivate you to become financially independent at a younger age.

To make the three money buckets go smoothly: To make your work easier and more frictionless, make sure you complete all transactions online. Recall that we are attempting to set up a mechanism that will divide our monthly money into the three buckets each month in less time than a minute. Although it might not seem simple at first, once you put this into practice, your life becomes more pleasant and your financial situation is in order. As soon as your salary appears in your account, divide it into the three buckets that were previously mentioned, then begin making purchases from the spending bucket. You can start planning your investing journey once it has been transferred into an investing account. Never consider transferring money from an investment account to a spending account; always use caution. After completing this activity, you become aware of your money-spending patterns during the first few months as you see how much you are spending on requirements and wants. You become aware of your ability to save as soon as you witness your investment account increasing.

You will quickly find out in a few months how much you could have saved if you had begun the same procedure a few months or years earlier. Many of you contend that this bucketing is unnecessary, that it is a time-consuming procedure, and that you should not spend valuable time on this exercise. However, behavioural economics can help with this. You are naming and labelling your three buckets of income as soon as you divide them up. This process is known scientifically as "Mental Accounting," and it will make it more difficult for you to take that money and spend it somewhere else. One instance of unconscious mental accounting we engage in when we spend money is the substantial credit card debt we have that we roll over, with an annual interest rate ranging from 30% to 40%.

On the other hand, we make regular monthly deposits that yield an interest rate of only about 6%. A more prudent and financially aware person would pay off the higher-interest loan before making any purchases. Regretfully, we are unable to view the two purposes of money through the same prism due to our mental accounting system. In summary, instead of doing monthly budgeting, which you may find tedious and uninteresting, you should establish a cash flow system and everything else would take care of itself.

How To Buy Your First House And Save Thousands Of Dollars

Our haven away from the chaotic world is our home. A house is a safe haven with plenty of emotional stimulation that one can use to relax, recharge, and regain composure. Our equilibrium is restored and we are able to create, flourish, love, and share in a home. Basic alarms go out when something goes wrong in our house. A large portion of errors are avoidable or predictable. I don't know about you, but I detest unpleasant surprises. A leaky roof is not fun. It's not fun to lose hot water. Not fun to have bats in the attic. Water leaks are inconvenient. Blowing fuses in electrical boxes is not fun. The response? a house examination.

A buyer's (and everyone else's, which I'll address later) house inspection helps protect them from suffering both financially and emotionally. I can relate tales of purchasers avoiding the inspection and then contacting an inspector afterwards to inquire as to why the gas heater blew up or why the deck collapsed off the rear of the house. The purpose of a home inspection is to reveal any surprises that may be there but are hidden from view before you purchase a property. Getting a home inspection will also save you money and stress in three additional situations: when you're building a home, when you're selling your house, and when you need a general evaluation after years of ownership. Wouldn't it be nice for you as the seller to be aware of what the buyer would see in their own report beforehand? Yes, I would. If there is a major issue (the surprise), you will then have the chance to address it and gain an advantage over your rivals.

Additionally, the majority of inspectors will charge you less for a seller inspection. I would suggest doing several inspections if you are building a house. The purpose of the inspections is to ensure that the builder does not inadvertently cause issues while building. The intention of builders is to create a high-quality, safe home for you, but I have witnessed a variety of mistakes, such as improperly built decks and structural piers that are not positioned perfectly beneath the building they are meant to support. I once went to a sizable construction site where an elevated walkway was being constructed. Halfway on and half off the concrete supports they had built the week before, I observed four walkway posts. I enquired about the situation with the contractor. "Well, when sitting on the supports, we made a calculation error.

We spilled them in the wrong spots and realised our mistake only after the posts were inserted. Right now, there is nothing we can do about it. The contractor cocked his head and gave me an embarrassed expression. I gave a throat clearing. Indeed, there is. Where new supports should be poured, you can pour them there. The walkway's fully supported poles were designed into the design. I gestured to one of the recently affixed posts to the outside part of a support pad. The post dangled half in the air. The contractor remarked, "Nobody will see it; it gets covered with a façade." "Anyway, this is all over-engineered." I gave a headshake. "That's even worse," I commented while taking pictures. I saw the contractor swivel his head from side to side and clench his eyes shut. "Aww. How disorganised. You're accurate. Alright. I pondered what may have happened if I hadn't inspected the job site that day as I was leaving.

Do not misunderstand me. I'm not claiming that builders intentionally commit mistakes. Although builders do their best, constructing a home or business building is a complex process that requires numerous crews to contribute to the final product. All it takes to cause mistakes to spread throughout the remainder of the building is a small number of inexperienced labourers and miscommunications. And last, once you move into the house, a home inspection is helpful. Five years later, have another inspection, and compare the conditions. What state are systems in? Have any issues surfaced? Throughout the next five to 10 years, what should you budget for? Do you have any safety concerns that you should be aware of?

Essential Information for Purchasers

You've found the ideal house. We've accepted your offer. Is this the house you believe it to be? "Yes" is the appropriate response to give your realtor when they inquire about getting a home inspected. These pointers will help you get the most out of your house inspection. Hire the top inspector. A skilled home inspector will identify significant issues and help you make decisions by providing you with an overview of the smaller concerns. Your inspector should have a great degree of experience and be properly licensed and/or certified in their field.

You might be given multiple names by your agent; you can either give them a call or look them out online. Since the cost of hiring the best and worst inspectors would probably be equal, why not optimise your return on investment? Some books on home inspections suggest hiring your own inspector rather than relying on the options your real estate broker provides. That's not what I agree with. I think a qualified and certified inspector will act morally and not hide flaws to help the agent close a deal. Does something like this ever occur? Though it's extremely uncommon in my experience, I expect that it does. An inspector runs the risk of facing consequences if they knowingly exclude flaws from a report. They are aware of that. Attend the inspection in person.

Because they believe they will annoy the inspector, 85% of prospective homeowners choose not to be present during the inspection. You will be informed by inspectors that this is untrue. Inform the inspector that you plan to attend the inspection's conclusion and that you anticipate some show and tell. This gives you the best of both worlds: a content inspector who is free to do their job without interruption, and your complete comprehension of the problems after they have finished. The inspector will give you their impression of the house overall while you are there. This is difficult to explain, and the written report does not convey this "sense." You will learn a great deal more information and information that is not readily apparent if you pay attention to the inspection. Set up a call with your inspector to go over the items if you are unable to be at the house while it is being inspected.

Over the phone, the inspector will provide you with information not included in the report. While it's not the same as being there, it's still far superior to reading the completed report alone and advising on upkeep. While not included in the official inspection, the majority of inspectors will inform you which parts of the house need routine maintenance and what those parts generally entail. Filter replacements, HVAC (heating, ventilation, and air conditioning) service intervals, unplugging the condensate line, etc. are a few examples. This is just one more justification for attending the walk-around. Utilise the inspector's knowledge and make notes. Request recommendations. Whom does the inspector suggest getting fixed? Additionally, you won't find this in the official report, but the inspector will employ a select group of highly skilled craftspeople; you ought to find out who they are.

Referrals are not given by inspectors since it can be interpreted as a conflict of interest. In person, they might provide you the names of their reliable craftsmen, but this is the proper protocol. Other inspections. Termite and WDO (Wood Destroying Organisms) inspections are one type of examination that your home inspector is not trained to perform. They are not authorised to report on infestations and what may be done about them, but they will notice and mention what they see. Homes are severely structurally damaged by termites. To check for termites and other pests and report on them, you should hire a pest professional. I have witnessed people have to demolish and rebuild portions of their homes after neglecting the termite check.

I found termite damage during one examination, but I couldn't tell if it was from recent or ongoing activity. I included this in the report, suggested hiring a professional pest inspector, and told the purchasers to hire a WDO professional to conduct a walk-around. "Our nephew Billy is going to do that," they said. "Is Billy a certified pest inspector?" I asked. "No, but he is aware of what to seek out." Before handing the report back, I underlined my recommendation to hire a pest control expert. The real estate agent that had handled the purchase drew me aside for a follow-up inspection a month later. "Do you recall the sixty-year-old house you examined, where you discovered termite damage in the basement?" "Yes, I definitely do." "The moment they moved in, three of the interior walls collapsed." "No!" Indeed. The pest inspection was never sent to them. I was in disbelief. Radon. If you plan to buy in a region of the country where the concentration of this radioactive gas is known to be high, get a radon inspection.

It comes in second place to cigarette smoking as a cause of lung cancer. Your realtor will be aware of the typical prices in the locations in which they are selling as well as whether it is advised. Refer to chapters 9 and 10.

Crucial Information for Sellers

In our minds, home inspections serve as the buyer's tool for determining whether or not to make the purchase. However, if you're selling a house, a home inspection can be a really useful tool. Wouldn't it be nice to know ahead of time what potential surprises might be hiding in your own house that you were unaware of? Pros and drawbacks are listed here. If you wish to steer clear of the last-minute surprises associated with a buyer's house inspection, it is a smart idea to have a seller's home inspection. Sometimes the results of an inspection startle both parties greatly.

Suddenly, there's effort, frustration, and a hint of insanity mixed in as the two sides argue about who will do what. Unexpected findings can occasionally ruin a contract. You have a better chance of keeping the sale if you can take care of things in advance. if you wish to promote the house with an advantage. Your home will stand out from the competition if you put in the extra work or add something unique to make it more appealing to purchasers. Getting an inspection shows prospective buyers that you are selling the house with all faults reported and that you take serious care of it. The house is already in decent shape.

Most likely, a home inspection will reveal certain things to you that you were not aware of. Even though they might be little, you can still take reasonable care of them. After that, the inspection report is used as a promotional tool. It might not be a smart idea to get a seller's home inspection if: You are aware that the home has several issues and would prefer not to find out more information about them. This may sound a little ostrich-like, but some sellers believe that it is preferable to keep flaws hidden and adhere to the "buyer beware" theory, even when they are aware that there could be consequences when conducting due diligence. The house is being sold exactly as is, with extremely major recognized faults. If you are the seller and you know the buyer will almost certainly be arranging their own inspection, there's not much use in listing all the flaws in the house in an inspection report if you intend to sell the house for the asking price, which is expensive.

You have already made the decision not to haggle even though you are aware that the buyer would be subject to an examination. You believe there might be a lot of radon in the house. The buyer might require you to install a ventilation system if it is determined that your home has a high level of radon (see chapter ten) and you choose not to install one to lower it. Although this makes sense, radon mitigation technologies are not cheap. Although it's up to you, I believe you would want to know the radon level. The following are additional benefits of seller-ordered inspections: The house is familiar to the seller. The history of any issues the house inspector discovers can be answered to his or her queries. When determining a reasonable asking price for the house, a home inspection will assist the seller in being more impartial. Before the house is available for visits, the seller will be informed of any safety concerns that are discovered within.

For seller inspections, the majority of home inspectors provide significant savings, and the inspection usually comes with a return visit and an updated report. Obtaining a seller's home inspection not only helps you sell your house faster and for more money, but it also typically lessens the stress that comes with the process. All of the information will be available to you, free from any surprises.

Essential Information for Owners

You've taken up residence. There were no unexpected findings in the inspection report. Now what? Load the box into a basement closet corner and place the report in the Home Sale Documents file folder. Or not? Not at all. You're losing the chance to prevent bank-breaking surprises if you throw the report away right away. Store the remaining information in a secure location and keep the report out of sight. Examine the report and make note of any information pertaining to the life and condition of the components.

You can find out how long this kind of water heater will endure, for instance, if your inspector certifies that your water heater is in good condition and you are aware that it is eight years old. After that, you can plan your budget for its replacement. You should be able to determine the estimated replacement cycles for your water heater, washing and dryer, refrigerators, decking, roofing, and other appliances, as well as your HVAC system, unless it is brand-new (which we'll address later). Although this stage takes time, once completed, you will be able to budget for future household spending. Rather than hearing someone exclaim, "Honey, there's no hot water," you will be able to pinpoint the precise moment of failure and be prepared with a backup plan. Even hot water heaters exhibit warning indications of imminent failure in the majority of units.

Make sure you set up a notebook or binder with the title "Home Components Service Life and Maintenance." Enumerate the parts and appliances. Mention their condition and include a replacement date.

The equipment will probably last longer than this day on the calendar, but at least you won't be taken aback and can afford the thing. A circumstance where an appliance lasts far longer than you anticipated is always a good thing. This is how refrigerators and washing machines often surprise us. I have no idea what dates to write here, you may be thinking. It's alright. Unbelievably, your inspector will typically be pleased to go through the report with you and assist you in identifying these items and dates if you phone them and ask for assistance. While you can offer to pay them to evaluate it, you should anticipate that most will do so as part of the inspection you just completed. You may get the life expectancy of materials, appliances, electronics, and roofs on the internet by searching for "home components life expectancy."

The International Association of Certified Home Inspectors also offers a free chart that may be downloaded as a PDF.1. These dates will benefit from routine upkeep. Combine routine prescribed maintenance with replacement planning and inspections if you truly want to cut costs. There won't be many financial shocks or cold water. Add service records, serial numbers, maintenance schedules, and other pertinent information to your notebook if you want to grow even more organised and ambitious. Although I like to keep the service manual attached to the appliance, I also photocopy the notebook's specifications and maintenance schedule. Whether you're looking for air filter sizes for the HVAC system or spark plugs for the tractor, having the specs on hand will save you a ton of time. Asking the home inspector for their assessment of the condition of each appliance is one proactive thing you can do when you have your house inspected.

Inform them that you're gathering data so you can avoid any surprises. Even though they state, "I can't predict anything for you," the inspector will respect you as a homeowner and may even express their ideas in person. It's probably a dead end to ask your inspector for recommendations on maintenance providers and repair firms. This is due to their desire to avoid becoming involved in a recommendation that would appear to have a conflict of interest or could perhaps backfire on them. Still, make the inquiry. They might know who they like to have current issues fixed. I've discovered that you run the danger of having a bad experience if the contractor information is out of date. This is due to the fact that many repair businesses' dependability and expertise fluctuate on a monthly basis.

Five years after you moved into your house, think about getting another home inspection. If at all possible, request a discount and the same inspector. They will recall you—yes, as inspectors, we keep in mind every house we've ever looked at. They will automatically give you a discount because they know you, which is a peculiar blessing (or curse—I'm not sure which to call it). There is also less pressure than when you inspect a house that is under contract. This five-year review will assist you in determining what aspects of your personal attention to detail need improvement. The price is certainly worth it. You will leave the next owner with an amazing amount of maintenance and component information if you decide to sell your house. For most purchasers, this indicates quality and attention to detail.

Essential Information for Agents

If you have any experience in the real estate industry, you are familiar with home inspections. You are aware that home inspections can be contentious, dramatic, and full of miscommunications, in addition to the other due diligence assignments you manage. Your patience and experience will be put to the test because this is the real world of selling real estate. Even the agents who have been around the block should find some of the tips I have to offer useful. We start with the rules, which vary from state to state but are often the same.

One piece of advice on home inspections that really sticks out to me as I read through the recommendations made by state boards or commissions is this one: brokers who represent potential tenants or buyers should encourage and advise their clients to order inspections, tests, and surveys for the properties they wish to buy or lease. They can also provide lists of qualified, licensed service providers for them to call and hire. Even if a client requests an inspection, test, or survey even though it is not necessary, a broker should never dissuade them from doing so. Inspections are a crucial component of the purchasing process for all buyers and, in certain cases, for tenants in business leasing agreements.

Furthermore, if a potential buyer declines to request an examination in an attempt to save money, it could have disastrous long-term effects.2. The majority of agents find no problems with this advice, and it makes sense. There are two places where things get tricky. The first is the way you select and suggest inspectors to clients; the second is the way inspectors manage client communications and reporting. Selecting and Endorsing Home Examiners Building relationships with real estate offices is something that home inspectors desire to do because these businesses can bring in a consistent flow of business.

Choose carefully. When you've chosen an inspector carefully, they can improve the effectiveness, dependability, and professionalism of your company.

Before giving out business cards and brochures to clients, do interviews with inspectors. If you weren't in the real estate industry, you wouldn't be skilled at making judgments about individuals. Spend enough time with the inspector so that you may be sure of your assessment. You should enquire about their years of inspection experience as well as their certifications and licences. Even if you're not hiring them to work directly for you, you want them to exhibit the same level of professionalism that you would if you were recommending them to a client. Just like you, home inspectors need to be completely truthful and conduct themselves with the greatest moral standards. Inspectors must have impeccable integrity because they spend hours by themselves in the houses of their clients. Observe inspectors' driving habits and professional demeanour while assessing them.

You are already aware of the fact that these traits convey a lot to your clients and represent your own professional demeanour and brand. Recognize that this is as good as it gets if the inspector interview does not go well. It's unlikely that the issues you find during the interview will disappear. If an inspector has a propensity of including little faults in reports that are actually rather significant, then even someone with their level of training and experience could cause chaos for everyone. It matters greatly how your inspector presents and discusses these concerns. You can find out how they respond to different kinds of problems. Asking them for an example report is also a good idea. Allow your customers to make their own decisions.

Additionally, let them know that they are free to select an inspector not on your list. Giving your client the option to study potential inspectors is something they will value, even if they decide not to. Should real estate agents recommend house inspectors they have a working relationship with, given their financial stake in the sale? It is not a conflict of interest, in my opinion, as long as the customer feels comfortable selecting an inspector in this manner—where the client is given options—and is aware that they are free to choose their own inspector. Agents are aware that a house with unreported flaws could be a ticking time bomb. Communications and Reporting The laws governing home inspections have led to a high degree of standardisation in home inspection reports across the United States. Although the layout is useful, your client may find the volume of detail daunting.

Verify that a sample report is clear and professional by asking to see it. The report's findings may be simple, but how they are presented may not always be clear-cut. I can tell you from my years of experience as an inspector that I overreacted to some of the issues I discovered in homes. This undesirable behaviour, sometimes referred to as the picky inspector syndrome, is typically the result of inexperience. New inspectors are afraid they'll overlook anything crucial. It's one thing when the inspector talks to you about the problems; it's another when they talk to the client about the problems. You will learn how these conversations go with your client after a few inspections. Inspectors must exercise restraint and calm because what they say to the client, the seller, if they are present, and any other agents at the property do carry significant weight. A lot of inspectors are quiet people. They might communicate more nervously as a result of this. Finding a technically skilled and knowledgeable inspector who can also effectively communicate with your clients in a reasoned and impartial manner is what you want. When deciding which inspectors to include on your list, this balance might be the most important quality to look for.

You should select inspectors with a great deal of experience. It's not that a novice inspector won't see things; rather, it's that they might find it difficult to tell what is and isn't significant. Give a novice a go by all means, but be aware that you might need to spend extra time explaining the significance of the flaws to the buyer. A major deck that needs to be replaced is not the same as a minor stair rail code infraction. An inspector's ability to identify genuine problems and lessen the drama surrounding smaller matters is enhanced by years of experience. Experience offers the necessary balance for both you and your client. When is it necessary to hire specialists? As generalists, home inspectors are not qualified to determine the cost of repairing major flaws or to rank the severity of a defect. In these situations, they will recommend a review by a professional. While hiring a professional is not required, it is a good idea if any item requires a technical analysis. The whole purpose of having the house examined is to evaluate the big faults, as these are the ones that can result in significant costs once the buyer moves in.

The ability to select inspectors who can distinguish between significant structural defects and less significant deviations is ultimately what matters. The reason inspectors are dubbed "picky" is not that they are overly meticulous, but rather that they are failing to make a sufficient distinction between what constitutes a significant and small infraction. A Few Additional Pointers Inspection reports contain so much boilerplate that it will seem as though it was prepared beforehand. This is inconvenient, but it's inevitable unless you believe the inspector genuinely overlooked inspection areas. You will frequently come across the same safety items, depending on the region of the nation in which your company is located. These are usually non-code problems (lint buildup in dryer vents, distance on railing verticals, structural faults on decks, and missing plumbing vents under sinks). You and the buyer can rely on the inspector to help you and the buyer understand these. Anything that poses a major risk to public safety should be reported. Urge the purchaser to show up for the inspection.

When discussing a home's shortcomings in person, it always goes more smoothly. An inspector would rather arrive early and do as much of the inspection on their own. This enables them to focus. When the inspection is almost over, you and the buyer can visit and conduct a walk-through. Encourage the buyer to phone the inspector for a recap if they are unable to attend the inspection. Although phone calls can be time-consuming, inspectors dislike them because they are less straightforward than reading reports and give them the opportunity to discuss details about a home that may not be covered in the report with the buyer. It's preferable for the seller to vacate the house while the inspection is taking place. It allows for increased focus and fewer uncomfortable situations.

Recall that home inspectors are not experts in their fields. No matter how sincere and harmless it seems, they shouldn't be recommending contractors or estimating repair expenses. This contradicts the advice I gave customers in the first chapter, which was to try asking for referrals in person as they might receive some helpful responses. Still, it's common to hear the reply, "I cannot refer others." The majority of this chapter has been devoted to discussing buyer inspections. Recall that sellers stand to gain from having an inspection done either before or soon after the listing. Seller inspections are frequently less expensive, come with an updated report to present prospective buyers, and come with a guarantee to return and re-inspect. Refer to What Sellers Need to Know, Chapter 2. Anticipating the surprises ahead of time is preferable to having them come as a shock.

Essential Information for Builders

Nothing compares to the excitement of creating and constructing a custom house. When they follow this path to their desire, the majority of people are happy and say they would do it again. However, in a private interview, these same individuals claimed to have run into a number of issues when building a bespoke home. They faced so many problems—from structural flaws to building delays and expense overruns—that they thought about abandoning the project or selling the house shortly after they moved in. Why is this happening? Everyone is prone to error. It's common and natural for designers, architects, builders, and owners to overlook things.

Finding the errors before the house is completed is crucial. Those of you who have had houses built may remember discovering problems with the residence after you moved in. A builder would tell you that this is all typical; considering the complexity of the systems in the home, there is no way they could have found and fixed every issue. "That comes with the job," a builder informed me. Home builders work really hard to construct the best possible home for you while avoiding errors. However, supervising subcontractors is a difficult task, and builders are busy people. The supervisor cannot constantly supervise the work at your home.

Even if the problems could be small—a hot cold water faucet, a broken light switch, a jammed window, a missing threshold seal, loose door hardware, the A problems list may represent the tip of a glacier, with more problems lying beneath the surface.

Ungrounded electrical outlets, upside-down plumbing pipe union installations, HVAC ductwork connected to the incorrect zones or cross-connected, missing return air ducts, undersized electrical circuits, oversized air compressors, and incorrect or absent weight-bearing structure are some of the major problems. I have personally witnessed all of these and more in my capacity as a contractor and former house inspector. This is a tale. The first time I drove into the garage, there was a raging snowstorm outside. There was a thick coating of snow covering the truck. A large piece of snow dropped to the ground as I climbed out and shut the truck cab door. We had asked the contractor to construct a drain in the two-car garage, so I figured the melting snow would flow off to the front of the structure.

I went upstairs and collapsed into bed, fatigued from a hard day and excited and thrilled to be in a newly constructed home. The new carpet, baseboards, and wood flooring were all soaked as I descended the stairs to the basement the following morning and discovered two inches of standing water throughout the garage and first floor rooms. I was horrified. Then, shockingly, I realised. The direction of the water is incorrect. The entire slab for the house was laid with the incorrect slope by the concrete contractor. It was three degrees sloping in the opposite direction from how it should have been—that is, toward the inside. If water cannot reach the drains, they are of no use. I found the shop vacuum in a hurry and started vacuuming water. Water in gallons upon gallons. When something like this happens, the only things you can do to fix it are to park outside during storms or keep a big shop vacuum close at hand.

A checklist and a thorough inspection could have helped to avoid this. Who was at fault? Mine. I should have checked for it, but I didn't. I should have discovered my mistake when I visited the jobsite during construction and saw rainwater gathering at the interior back of the basement. At the time, it was just a half-formed, persistent thought. I ought to have paid closer attention. Even though our city's building inspectors are highly skilled and knowledgeable, they only examine a limited range of construction components. Building code provisions are meant to protect us, and building inspectors take note of them. Since they are not looking for it and it is not on their checklist, they are likely to overlook patio and garage drainage slopes. What then do you do? There are two options available to you.

The first option is to defer to the builder and trust them to find the mistakes. Alternatively, you might employ a certified house inspector to conduct several inspections while the construction is underway. I suggest doing an inspection, at the least, before the foundation is poured, before the drywall is installed, and right before your walk-through with the builder. Your own punch list will incorporate the inspector's list. Additionally, I advise you to employ a structural building engineer and have them conduct an inspection right before drywall and concrete are installed.

A list of problems will be given to you by both experts. You should be happy that you gave the builder the punch list details because it's your money and your contract. Since they are making every effort to detect every problem on their own, it makes their job easier. Nonetheless, some builders refuse to permit independent examinations. If an inspector discovers something amiss, they see it as a critique of their professionalism. Go with a different builder, is my recommendation. It is best to obtain as many eyes as possible on the project. Would you rather wait and hope for the best, or pay a few thousand dollars throughout the building process (less than one percent of the average cost of a custom-built home, which is between $350K and $600K)? My experience with home inspections has shown me that investing the additional funds will be worthwhile.

Permit me to say that again. The additional money spent on independent inspections will pay off, based on what I've learned about home inspections. Construction Agreements Include a provision in your building contract allowing you to employ third-party inspectors. Additionally, mention that the builder has committed to reviewing the inspection suggestions and paying for the correction of any faults for which they are accountable. Make a list of all the clauses that state "variable" or "depends on" in your builder's contract. These are the kinds of things that a fixed-cost contract does not fix. These locations are the ones that catch you off guard. Any builder who has begun a custom home understands that unexpected things happen. These might range from weather-related delays that cause damage to already completed work to inadvertent mistakes made by subcontractors.

Plan mistakes, footings, and excavation are common areas where overruns occur. To be prepared, ask your builder to assist you in estimating the worst-case cost of these items. If all goes according to plan, you will be happy. Verify the materials list again. Are you positive you selected all the appropriate appliances and fixtures? illumination? Where are the wall switches located? Examine these in great detail. Get a second opinion from someone else before you look at the plans and lists if you have been too attached to them to remain impartial. It won't be the builder's fault if, after moving in, you discover that the bathroom fittings aren't what you selected. How do you suppose I discovered that? Make a note of the things the builder needs to do. They will be grateful that you are taking care of your house because a knowledgeable owner makes their job much easier.

With few superintendents, many prosperous builders have dozens of homes under construction at any given moment. It's possible they don't work on the project every day. Find out from them the preferred format and frequency for the issues list. The home's builders will provide a one-year warranty. Most new owners just move in and don't think about the warranty until something obvious breaks. This is an error. You should email the builder a comprehensive report of any problems you discover, which you will undoubtedly do. This facilitates scheduling for the builder. Items may include windows that are stuck, loose toilet tanks, caulked gaps, vinyl floor lifting, loose grout, nails popping through walls, and balanced heating and cooling vent adjustments, among other things.

You will avoid the usual financial surprises and receive a far higher quality home when you take the time to actively manage your custom home project with the builder and the additional independent inspections. Who is Building This? Do you undertake the construction? An impartial inspector is even more important if you are building your own house or serving as your own contractor. Make an appointment with your house inspector well before the start of work. Examine the plans and find out what inspections they believe need to be done during the process. Participate in the examinations. Enumerate the items they discover. It is inevitable for even the most diligent subcontractors to overlook something. Who bears the ultimate cost of errors? You do, unless the subcontractor is notified and you catch it just in time.

You risk paying an additional 15–20 percent for the house or having to live with errors that are irreversible if you choose not to have these inspections because you are too busy or don't want to hire someone to help you. Particularly Important Things Your builder will work as efficiently as possible to keep costs associated with your project to a minimum. I've discovered a couple places where they try to make you think certain things are "extra" when they ought to be normal. Go over your contract in detail. The Energy Recovery System (ERV), which facilitates air exchange within the house, and ventilation to the outside for gas and cooking equipment are two frequently disregarded items. Even in rural areas, indoor air pollution is significantly higher than outside air pollution, according to the Environmental Protection Agency (EPA). This is due to the fact that all human activities, including breathing and cooking, lead to poor air quality in populated areas.

To reduce harmful health effects, the EPA advises residential buildings to have an air exchange rate of at least 0.35 air changes every hour, but not less than 15 cubic feet of air per minute per person. I discovered there was no air exchanger (ERV) in the newly built house I was inspecting for a client. The builder asked me why. "It's another thousand dollars and the owner didn't ask for it," was his response. Poor response! Since modern buildings are already so tightly constructed, neglecting the air exchanger invites condensation and lower-than-ideal indoor air quality. A Blower Door Test may be necessary in certain states prior to a residence receiving a Certificate of Occupancy (CO). This easy-to-do test gauges the efficiency of the house by determining how airtight it is. Oddly enough, though, an air exchanger (ERV or HRV) is not necessary.

Verify that every gas appliance is properly vented to the outdoors. Indoor fireplaces and cooking are two major sources of indoor air pollution. Installing air vents requires more labour for builders, so make sure the contract details the kinds and quantity of vents to be installed in the house. Cooking and gas appliance vents ought to go outside rather than inside.

Selecting an Inspector

We are passionate about our work. Every examination is a mystery-solving journey. We adore every aspect of it, even the parts that are difficult to perceive as nobody else looks there. We take greater pride in our capacity to identify what is right and wrong when things get harder. While we appreciate well-maintained properties, we get a thrill when we uncover a major issue that could have bitten the next owner. We want to think we're helping them avoid financial ruin and trauma. Finding a property is actually our first challenge. Following the GPS, I have found myself in quarries and on little, one-way roads that lead to dense forests, valley creek crossing paths, and mountaintops. I've visited cities with skyscrapers so tall that the GPS was unable to locate them.

We take pleasure in providing briefings and problem interpretation for our clients. When a report is put together and sent to the client, we feel satisfied. It's a physically taxing profession. On an average examination, we carry heavy ladders, fit through narrow spaces into the unknown, and cover four miles on foot. We have to deal with foxes, rats, rabbits, skunks, raccoons, wild dogs, spiders, and snakes. When we don't have the gate key, we occasionally have to hike onto a property. We operate in all types of weather. Among the many tools and equipment we carry, our cameras and binoculars are the most crucial. The training is extensive. The day concludes with actual home inspections following a week of theory and practical instruction. Before I became a lone inspector, I worked as an apprentice for six months under another inspector. I have yearly recurring training and have passed three tests.

Home inspectors: What Are They? There is a lack of clarity on the duties and authority of house inspectors. They are frequently confused with appraisers, building inspectors, and pest inspectors. Let's dispel this misunderstanding. A property's zoning, set-back restrictions, permits, and code compliance are examined by a municipal or city building inspector. Before a transaction, some communities demand this evaluation. A building inspector will conduct periodic inspections of newly constructed homes to ensure compliance with building rules and other municipal requirements. In contrast, a home inspector is an independent contractor licensed by the state (if applicable) and does not work for the city. Any state does not require a home inspection report when purchasing a residence.

A house inspector inspects a lot more ground than an appraiser or an inspector of building codes. Home inspectors are generalists with knowledge of plumbing, heating and air conditioning, building materials, construction, and electrical design. They are knowledgeable about safety procedures, deck systems, building codes, and component life expectancy. Although they are capable of replacing your water heater or building you a deck, their area of expertise is inspection. They are excellent at identifying the issue and providing an explanation. Despite the fact that many contractors are also house inspectors, a general contractor is not the same as a home inspector. Zoning compliance, permits, setback restrictions, homeowner association standards, and fire sprinkler testing are not tasks performed by home inspectors. The differences between home appraisers and home inspectors are also unclear.

An appraiser gathers data about the house and does data analysis to determine the property's market value. They gather square footage, the costs of nearby residences, and information on past sales prices. Their assessment and opinion, derived from the data, are reflected in the report they create. Usually, the lending institution hires appraisers, and the buyer pays for the report. If they have up-to-date information and photos, they might or might not actually enter the house. How to Choose the Qualifications of a Professional Home Inspector. A significant body that certifies home inspectors should have your inspector on file. The International Association of Certified Home Inspectors (InterNACHI) and the American Society of Home Inspectors (ASHI) are the most well-known.

Strict requirements apply to membership, and the organisations offer continuing education. Also, your inspector might hold a state licence. In the United States, 35 states will require home inspectors to hold a licence as of 2021. Experience. Everybody had to start someplace. I made a lot of blunders in the early years of my own home inspection business, overlooked things that I should have noticed, and raised concerns about things that I shouldn't have. Hire a home inspector with at least two years of experience—take my advice and learn from it. It's much better after five years. Either way, the total amount you pay will be the same. The most crucial skill for a licensed inspector to possess is experience. A lot of states that have licensing requirements also mandate yearly refresher courses. An added benefit is that it keeps inspectors informed. thorough reporting. Request a URL to an example report from your potential inspectors.

The detailed inspection report, which may consist of over twenty pages, is very significant. More is preferable. Seek for material that is straightforward to read and has explanations for any difficulty spots highlighted.

The inspector will send you a link to their website or send you a copy in PDF format. reputation. You can use social media to learn about previous customers' experiences with a certain inspector. You want an inspector who is "thorough," but you don't want one who is "picky." Since your real estate agent frequently interacts with inspectors, they might be of assistance in this regard. Agents won't put up with an inspector who takes their time pointing out little details while ignoring the important ones. They also don't pick the "easiest" inspectors to close deals with. In addition to wanting you to enjoy your new house, agents also want to maintain their own good names. Price. Never bargain over the cost. Inspections will be approximately the same cost in any given geographic location.

The cost of a house inspection will pay for itself in preventative maintenance, prospective sales revenue, and averting major costs. savings. Even though I recently advised against haggling, it doesn't harm to ask nicely for a discount. The worst case scenario is that the inspector will reject your request. They may occasionally respond in the affirmative. Agree. Prior to the inspection, make sure your inspector provides you with a comprehensive agreement. Examine the specifics. It's the only thing you can do if something goes wrong. Make sure you are aware that your inspector does not look for termites and is unable to see through walls. sophisticated instruments. Find out from your inspector how the crawlspace and roof will be examined. They ought to respond to cameras and visual inspection. Advanced tools are not necessary, but they could be useful in difficult-to-reach places. Particularly helpful are remote-control robots for the crawlspace and drones for the roof. They both offer a quality video feed and can be operated with a smartphone. When I was inspecting, I wished I had them. webpage.

Professional websites are a must for competent house inspectors. The website has all the information you would need, including links to social media and a sample report. You'll probably be sent to the website so you can pick up your report as well. Due to its ease of use and speed, this system is excellent. Social Networks. Your inspector most certainly has a Facebook page and accounts on other media-sharing websites. Check for the links and icons on their website. Go through what others have to say. I liked sharing anonymous photos of major flaws I found when inspecting, just to give people an idea of what we do. I received a lot of traffic, from the mouldy, opaque swimming pool to the structural joists removed to move a wall.

Top Five Inspection Myths

Everything is covered by a home inspection. Untrue. Even though a home inspector might spend hours on an inspection, there are many things they are blind to. They are unable to move furniture to inspect it, ascertain whether there is a problem within the walls, or predict whether a malfunction will occur soon after the purchasers move in. Specialist inspections are not permitted for most house inspectors. These inspections cover things like septic and well inspections, mould detection, pool and spa inspections, and infestations by termites and other insects. When they discover anything alarming, home inspectors will alert you so you may arrange for an appropriate expert to assess it.

Your presence during the inspection will be unsettling to the inspector. Untrue. Although it's true that house inspectors are a bit of an aloof, nerdy group of people who would really rather be left alone, the reality is that if you show up for the inspection, the likelihood of miscommunication and misunderstandings will be much decreased. Attending the inspection will also provide you excellent insight into the systems in the house. No matter how detailed the report is, inspectors will be able to tell you significantly more in person than they can in a report. Getting a briefing and showing up at the conclusion of the inspection will be the best of both worlds. Since the buyer will receive an inspection, there is no purpose for the seller to obtain one of their own.

Myth: Getting a home inspected before listing can be especially helpful for sellers. You will fall behind if you wait and rely on customers to notify you of errors. Refer to What Sellers Need to Know, Chapter 2. It is not necessary to get a home inspection before purchasing a newly constructed or recently renovated home. Myth:

Every home, no matter how old—one month, one hundred years, or freshly renovated—benefits from an examination. Particularly newly constructed and custom-built homes have a long list of errors and oversights that should be found and fixed before you move in. After the examination, the inspector will rate the quality of your home and give you an opinion on whether or not to buy. Myth. Anyone would desire this, of course. The report you get will be extremely detailed, but it won't give the house a grade.

The inspector is not going to give you advice on whether or not to purchase the house. This is due to a number of factors. The inspector is simply examining what is readily apparent and reachable, to start. The second is that not every system and device in the house will be graded by the inspector, who is a generalist. This is merely one of the reasons you should be present at the inspection. The inspector has a lot to say that you will find quite beneficial. You will gain a far greater "feel" for the home from an inspector than from simply reading the written report, even though they will make every effort to be totally objective when they discuss the house with you.

Using the Report

I love aeroplanes. A few summers back, I presented a talk about building your own aeroplane at an airshow. Someone approached me after the session and announced they were going to buy an old experimental aircraft that same day. I questioned them about who was checking out the craft before they bought it. "It flew in here to the show so it must be fine," they claimed, indicating that they would be forgoing the inspection. This is like claiming that since a house's roof doesn't leak, everything else inside must be good if you're buying a house. Get an inspection whether you are purchasing a house or an aeroplane. The amount you pay will be insignificant compared to what you may have to pay to have significant flaws fixed. Here's how to make financial savings with an inspection report.

Let go of the minor details. Fixing a stuck window is possible. One can fix a leaky faucet. Attic insulation that is missing can be added. Even better, you can request repairs from the vendor. Although they don't have to, they frequently will in order to please you. Go to the Major things portion of the report after skipping over these things. Typically, these appear first in the report's list and/or summary. The seller is required by law in the majority of states to disclose to you any material flaws in the house (referred to as a "material defect disclosure"). This hardly ever occurs. This could be because the seller is unaware of it rather than necessarily trying to hide it. I've searched dozens of basements and discovered furnaces that were recalled due to carbon monoxide concerns, but the owners were fortunately unaware of this. Leaks of carbon monoxide into a house can be deadly.

The important things are the ones that will either have a substantial financial impact on you or put your safety and wellbeing at danger when you're at home. Though they are useful to have, every home contains the maintenance and repair supplies. A few last things to consider. The first is that a house inspection report does not need to be used for any purpose. In order to help the seller and buyer assess the state of the house and avoid any unpleasant surprises, the report includes the recommendations of a certified and experienced inspector. The second piece of advice is to trust your real estate agent's judgement. They are professionals who have done this often and can offer you well-considered, precise counsel.

Further Exams

Since your home inspector is a generalist, if they notice something that worries them, they will suggest that you contact a specialist. For instance, they can advise getting a septic or sewer examination if they believe the plumbing is operating slowly. List these suggestions in a list. In the long run, it might save you money even though you are not required to work with any of the specialists. I'll outline the most popular specialised examinations and tests and let you know if your inspector is qualified to do them. I'll also offer my assessment on the significance of obtaining a certain inspection. Pay close attention to what your inspector has to say. Their advice is derived from years of expertise. Infestations of pests and termites.

Typically, an inspector is not authorised to conduct an inspection for wood-destroying organisms (WDOs). Hire a pest control expert. Strongly advised for each and every home inspection. Termites can inflict significant structural damage by hiding their damage behind walls and foundations. Radon. may be carried out by house inspectors. You should absolutely have this examination if you want to build or purchase a home in a region of the nation where radon exposure is frequent. To read about radon, turn to the following chapter. For less than fifty bucks, you can get a kit and do this test on your own. Aqua. Home inspectors are able to perform this test, but the sample is forwarded to a lab that tests water or sent to the local health department. Suggested if the house has well water.

A complete chemical analysis panel can be costly and need weeks to complete; basic tests can be completed at a low cost in a few days. By obtaining a water sample and sending it to a lab, you can also perform the test on your own. Companies that drill holes can handle both the testing and sending the sample to a lab. If nothing else, you ought to obtain a cheap test for bacterial contamination, which is part of the basic panel. This checks your water for the presence of coliform and E. Coli germs. It is unacceptable for a water sample to include any amount of faeces. Sewer or Septic? not carried out by house examiners. Not advised until an issue seems to be present.

Inspections of septic systems need to be done every three to five years. Alarm Frameworks. not carried out by house examiners. The organisation is able to conduct the inspection if the alarm is professionally monitored. A fee might apply or it might not. Lawn Sprinkler systems. could be covered by a house inspection or not. A plumber is able to inspect and fix. Air Quality Inside. Not advised unless there is a valid reason to be concerned, such as the discovery of mould. Get a recommendation from your house inspector. Additionally, the Environmental Protection Agency's website (EPA.gov) offers information on indoor air quality. Mould. Not advised unless the house inspector finds a problem. Allergy reactions to mould can result in upper respiratory symptoms such as runny nose, cough, sneezing, wheezing, and shortness of breath. Visit the National Organization of Remediators and Mould Inspectors to locate an inspector.

To identify the type of mould, a mould inspection uses air and surface sampling in addition to testing for moisture incursion and humidity levels. To locate damp or cold patches behind walls and make recommendations about how to eliminate them, inspectors utilise thermal imaging instruments. The Institute of Inspection Certification and Restoration Certification (IICRC) shall certify mould inspectors. Inspection of Structures. Not advised unless the house inspector finds a problem. If they notice something, they will direct you to a professional engineer. chimney.

As part of your examination, the home inspector will visually evaluate the firebox and the chimney components from the roof and the attic. They will advise a chimney sweep if they discover damaged mortar, creosote buildup (a residue from burning wood), or flue flaws. When a fire starts in the flue, it can spread swiftly, destroying the entire house. spas and swimming pools. Suggested if your house has a spa or pool. Although they can recommend a testing business, your home inspector will not do these specialist examinations. contaminates. Homes built before 1978 may have lead (in paint), asbestos (in insulation), and other pollutants. Request a referral to a risk assessor from your inspector if you have any concerns. Go to EPA.gov.

Facts About Radon

I've put together a quiz to liven up the conversation about a colourless, odourless, radioactive gas because it can be dull at times. Should you already be an expert on radon, you'll breeze through the test. What makes you need to worry? Because different amounts of the gas radon can be detected inside homes. Radon, second only to smoking cigarettes in terms of contributing to lung cancer, can cause significant quantities. During the day, radon gas is analogous to solar radiation and is emitted from space. Is it true or false? Untrue. The naturally occurring radioactive decay of uranium in rock, soil, and water produces radon, which is released into the atmosphere. Tasteless, odourless, and colourless is radon. Water contains radon as well.

Radon testing is a difficult and time-consuming procedure that requires a professional to complete. Is it true or false? Untrue. At your neighbourhood home improvement store, a test kit can be purchased for less than fifty dollars. You just hang the kit in your house and mail it to a lab for the test, which takes a few days to complete. Local county or city health departments occasionally offer free test kits. A radon level of more than 4.0 pCi/L is regarded as dangerous. Is it true or false? Indeed. The unit of measurement for radon in the air is picocuries per litre of air, or pCi/L. Although many experts recommend 2.0 pCi/L or less is much better, levels less than 4 pCi/L are seen to be safe.

In the United States, radon exposure results in times as many deaths annually as drunk driving. Is it true or false? Indeed. According to EPA.gov, drunk driving results in over 10,000 annual fatalities whereas radon causes over 20,000 deaths from lung cancer. Your home's top floor will have the highest radon test results since the

Gas ascends. Is it true or false? Untrue. Radon enters your house through the lowest level from the earth, but barriers like flooring, insulation, and plastic can slow it down. Radon can occasionally be reduced to safer levels by merely caulking air leaks and slab and foundation gaps. There is not a trace of radon in the air outside your house. Is it true or false? Untrue.

According to EPA.gov, the average outside level is actually.4 pCi/L, or picocuries per litre. States have different levels of radon, and places with mountains may have higher levels than others. Is it true or false? Indeed. Radon has been detected in every state in the union, despite regional variations in radon levels. I have examined residences in North Carolina's mountains that had readings above 35 pCi/L. That's true, 35 is more than eight times the permissible limit. You will have to vacate the property and have the building remedied if radon testing in your house reveals levels over what is deemed safe. Is it true or false? Untrue. The good news is that it is not very expensive to lower the radon levels in your house if necessary.

The first line of defence is typically a vent and fan system, which will reduce the radon to tolerable levels more than 75% of the time. Can you request that a seller fix their house if elevated amounts are discovered? You certainly can. In fact, you want to inquire; in the worst case scenario, you might be able to negotiate a lower selling price and arrange for the remediation to be completed prior to your move in. What was your performance? Visit www.epa.gov and www.radon.com, the websites of the Environmental Protection Agency, to learn more.

Real Stories

The collective tales of home inspectors are astounding. They can be heartwarming, spooky, or disturbing. Going to recurrent training with other inspectors and meeting in the bar at the end of the day is what I enjoy doing the most. Stories never cease to amaze us. They include things like jewels piled inside HVAC ducts, fuse panels with pennies installed, basements without stairs, and hydraulic vehicle jacks supporting floor timbers and doors. Crawlspaces: I crawl into the spaces beneath houses while fully clothed in Tyvek coveralls. Even the smallest crawlspaces can reveal important information about the state of the house. It's also among the riskiest locations you may visit.

It requires extreme caution and ongoing attention to avoid everything from brown recluse spiders to hibernating bears to a range of venomous snakes. To protect myself from various moulds, bacteria, viruses, and spores, I also wear a Plexiglas face shield and an airtight mask with breathing filters in addition to the Tyvek suit. I sometimes feel like the alien dude from the movie Alien. I was once checking out a big cabin in the highlands. There was a tiny, unimproved gravel road that led to the cabin, which was located in a secluded area seven miles away. As I made my way through the thick forest and reached an elevation of five thousand feet on my GPS, I couldn't help but wonder why anyone would choose to live so far away. As I approached the large, empty cabin, the solution became clear to me. From the front porch, a multicoloured vision of gently pastel-shadowed mountain ranges stretched out to the horizon, set against the deep forests.

I took in the breathtaking beauty of the early morning scene while standing silently on the deck. A garden of native perennials including blue and gold lantana and daisies was greeted by an unevenly mowed lawn. However, nobody resides here. I questioned why it had just garnered attention. I put aside my reflections and went to work, putting everything I needed—including bear spray, screwdrivers, and cameras—on my inspector's belt. I looked around the internal chambers and walked the roof before looking for the crawlspace's exterior entrance. I discovered it facing the woods at the back of the cabin. The door hung unfastened, secured with a padlock and hasp. Alright.

That being said, the entrance was really tiny. Not remarkable. How the larger inspectors entered via these doors baffled me. I could fit through these openings since I weighed a hundred and eighteen pounds and was just five feet seven inches tall. They stay outside. I unlocked the door by taking the padlock off of the hasp. Shadows. I slithered onto the dirt floor from the twenty-inch square aperture. I raised the spotlight. Tiny cobweb strands and dust particles drifted in the arc of yellow light. Just inches above my head, in the gaps between the beams, large wolf spiders held their ground. I was aware that snakes loved to sleep where the insulation had fallen to my left. The sound of distant water dripping was the only sound to break the silence.

I crept silently past the insulation pile on my belly and made my way to the dark pool of water at the far end. I slithered over bits of plastic sheeting, mouse carcasses, and dropped insulation squares. I noticed movement to my right out of the corner of my eye. I was shocked to see three pairs of reflecting yellow circles move and then halt when I rotated my light beam. Coops. Something was chittering and snarling. I could see my flashlight's yellow cast starting to wane. Then I heard the screeching metal of the padlock clasp closing and the tiny door behind me crash shut. Captured. My body felt a wave of ice cover me from head to foot while I struggled to comprehend what was going on. I could feel the ceiling beams getting closer to me. Such a small area.

Leave now! I was having trouble breathing. I started screaming at the top of my lungs out of instinct. "Hey! Hey!" I spun around and began to slide and crawl in the direction of the small entrance. I hoped I hadn't startled the sleeping snakes by giving the insulation pile a wide berth. When I got to the door, I banged on it with the hefty light's back end. I wanted my heart to stop racing so I could think of a way out. I perceived a male voice. "Hey, what?" Is someone inside of that? "Yes, the house examiner! Kindly let the door open. "All right, now hang on. Oh my. The door sprang open and I heard metal on steel. I darted through that gap so quickly that I frightened the man, who took several steps back, stumbled over a fallen limb, and collapsed into a heap of leaves. He was swaying back and forth. He exclaimed, "You look like an astronaut."

I took off my headgear and inhaled deeply, understanding that I now knew what claustrophobia was. I was staring at the man. Oh my, I apologise. I had no idea you were inside. As the yard person, I noticed that the crawl door was open. You don't want any animals inside, do you? With trepidation, he laughed. I answered, "Of course, but you sure did give me a scare." "I didn't think anyone would be here." I apologise for it. I would have left the hatch open if I had known. "It's all good that it ends well." I made the decision to conclude the crawl space inspection. The leak over the black pool would be visible in my images. Water Operations I told the agent over the phone, "I can't inspect the home if the water isn't on." Yes, that's correct. For the examination, I will ask the owner to switch it on. After a few days, I got out of the truck and put on my jacket.

It was a very cold breeze. With two-story tall pillars at the entrance, the six-thousand-square-foot villa stood elegantly against the backdrop of the golf course. A palace. As soon as the agent arrived, I pulled up my coat collar and started my walk-around outside. We walked into the home's foyer when the agent unlocked the grand front door. The thick cream-coloured carpet underneath us appeared to sink our feet into it and had a rotting scent. Before moving, we took a look around. I said, "Do you hear something?" Not at all. How come? "It must be in my head. Never mind. I'll work my way down from the top floor. Alright. Here in the entryway, I'll plug in and finish up some work.

The place needs to be ventilated because it has a deathly odour. Even after climbing the enormous, curved staircase beneath a complex crystal chandelier, I couldn't shake the feeling that there was something loud inside the house. I couldn't tell if it was gurgling or humming. I was testing outlets and fixtures when I forgot about it. I observed that there was little water pressure. I decided to go outside and perform a pressure test. The house was outfitted with everything needed. I saw oil paintings on the walls, canopied beds, little figurines, and antiques. It makes sense that the agent desired to be there for the examination. Every electrical and water fixture on the second level tested OK, with the exception of the low water pressure. Plus, the scent was better up there.

I heard the sound once more as I descended the Gone with the Wind stairs. "I sense something right now. I'm going to investigate it. To the agent, I said. "Come on, I'll let you know if you hear anything," Turning the corner, we entered the enormous living room with its eighteen-foot ceiling and proceeded towards the kitchen. "Yeah, it sounds like something," the agent responded. It was an unsettling sound. It made a swishing, lapping, and gurgling sound. We paused and exchanged glances. Our gaze strayed to the room's corners. The sound carried into the corridor. I crossed the kitchen to a door in the corner. This ought to take you to the basement. After giving the agent one more glance, I opened the door. I was terrified to look, but I knew what it was as soon as the sound burst forth. I gestured for the agent to approach. I fully opened the door and turned on the light switch. We both let out a collective "Oh my God!".

A quarter of the way up the carpeted basement stairway was a murky pool of water. Under the bottom wall, waves gurgled. There were bubbles curling up from below, items floating in the water were slamming against one other, and there were hissing noises. After letting my inspection belt fall to the kitchen floor, I dashed into the living room, out the front door, and onto the street. I found the supply handle and switched it off as I ran into the well shed. When I got back to the house, I saw the agent, who was pale and talking on the phone, seated on a kitchen stool. She constantly shook her head. I made my way back up the basement stairs. Since the water supply was turned off, the pool appeared to be calmer.

As I was taking pictures, the agent approached me to end the call. What you're looking at below is the equivalent of a household swimming pool below ground. I answered, "I'm assuming a burst pipe that's been going on in the basement for days." She said, "Nobody is going to believe this." "It makes sense why the water pressure was low," I answered. The Cavern of Obsidian During home inspections, common doors sometimes reveal something unexpected. There are doors that go to rooms, doors that lead to a shadowy space, and doors that are oddly locked. You can occasionally acquire all three. I was doing an inspection of a big vacation house on a broad, swift-moving creek north of Cashiers. It was a maze of waterfalls, curves, and boulders. I would have taken out my lunch box and stopped by the creek if I hadn't been on a timetable. The scenery was brilliant and spectacular.

The driveway was steep and narrow, ending at a massive gate that led to the house. The agent gave me a working remote, and the gates opened slowly on grumpy hinges. The home features breathtaking floor to ceiling windows and was exquisitely fashioned into the side of granite and quartz ledges. The house was only a few thousand square feet on the ground, but two floors loomed above the ground, making the most of the extremely steep property. The house was empty after going through a foreclosure. How unfortunate. My ideal home. There were no irregularities found during the initial portion of the first floor inspection. As I began my ascent to survey the second story, I came upon a door secured by a deadbolt. Most of the time, owners are attempting to safeguard something when you see anything like this.

Usually, I would write in the report that I was unable to enter the closet or room, but since the bank was the owner in this instance, I didn't think they were aware of the locked door. I picked up the phone and called the real estate agent. She said, "I'll give the bank a call." The phone rang three minutes later. "That door is unlocked by anyone's key. I would advise you to go in and report anything you find if we did. Are you able to select it? "I'm not a locksmith," I answered. "No problem, I'll mention that I had to skip it in my report." I'm intrigued. I touched the top of the door trim, where I keep a secret key, with my hand. Something with Velcro adhered to the edge caught my fingers. a key. I tried turning the lock after inserting the key. It was successful! I turned the knob and let the door open, leaving the key in the tumbler. A dark emptiness. I took out my flashlight and pointed it in that direction. There was a circular staircase made of black metal. I felt like Nancy Drew right now. I took my time descending the small set of steps. Next, I heard the door above close. Startled, I raised my head. The door featured a self-closing spring, I noticed.

Does it also lock itself? I pondered. All I needed was to be stranded in the far-off house, in an unfamiliar chamber with a round stairway that led to no one knowing where. Taking out my phone, I checked to see if I still had a signal. Not a single bar. I was worried and wanted to know if I could escape. I walked back up the stairs and spun around to make sure the door had not locked behind me. I grabbed the knob. Secured. How did you end up in this predicament? I looked for a light switch on the wall with my flashlight. After finding it, I turned it on. The landing was filled with light. Upon examining the door lock, I observed that the non-operating lock was the lower one, the knob lock. I extracted multiple business cards and gently inserted them into the door frame, thus disengaging the lock. I exhaled a breath of calm. To go back out, I reached around the door and turned the lock lever to the vertical position.

If I should continue exploring, I pondered. Indeed. I turned off the landing and down the stairs once again. I could hear the sound of water halfway down. When I got down the bottom, there were two additional doors set into the walls and a roughly six-by-six-foot space with an uneven stone floor beneath my feet. I searched the area for a switch. It was on the wall across from me. The room was illuminated when I flicked the switch. The fact that the walls were etched into the cliff astounded me. There was a small closet with an electrical box in it.

Like the one upstairs, the other door was secured with a deadbolt. "Oh! I stated to myself aloud, "I left the key upstairs. "Shoot, I have to climb back up to retrieve it." To get it, I ascended the circular staircase once more. Was I really getting into more than I could handle? I'm intrigued that I've made this far. I turned around and descended the steps to the locked door.

I got the door open with the key in its holder. Water trickled down the tiny passageway's walls, which were made of granite hewn from the cliff face with an obsidian-coloured hue. I could see the ridges left by the blasting caps. I was feeling uneasy. Do I need to continue? I carefully made my way over the rough dirt road, noticing that the walls were getting smaller.

down the slick hillside. My illumination picked out a hefty, closed door that was in the way, and I heard a sort of hissing sound. My intellect said, Go back. No, I'm just interested. The same key operated this massive door once more. The hissing sound turned out to be water as soon as I pressed on the door. The rusty hinges of the door creaked. I walked carefully down the cavern passage, and the sound of the water got louder.

My curiosity got the better of me, and I heard the old door crash behind me. I froze, aiming my light towards the entrance and back up the passage. Fantastic. I thought, I hope I can go back out. Nobody would know if something were to happen to me down here. I took another dozen hesitant steps when the tunnel wall abruptly turned ninety degrees. On the wall across from us, light spilled. I took the next move. I was facing the waterfall that I could see from inside the house. I let out a deep sigh, realising that I had been holding my breath. I took a deep breath of the chilly, humid air and felt a wave of relief rise up through me. As I took pictures, I thought to myself, I simply need to get out of here now. "This will not be believed by anyone," I said to myself. Attic Features After being unoccupied for a year, the modest two-story cottage caught the attention of a potential buyer. From the exterior, everything appeared OK, and I completed my first walk-around inspection in search of any issues.

As I was finishing up my inspection of the HVAC compressor by the house, I felt a few heavy drips fall on my head. I took a look around. There was no rain on this beautiful day. I looked up after that. Another big, wet drop struck me in the face, and this time I saw a two-inch PVC tube protruding from the second-story soffit. How in the world? I took some telephoto photos and noted the location. I set up a ladder and ascended to the roof. I couldn't get to the spot where I'd noticed the PVC pipe since one side was really steep. When I enter, I'll investigate. I moved through the rooms before arriving at the attic. There are houses with stairs, houses with big square access panels, and houses with little square access panels. That day, I had the good fortune to find a little access panel hidden within a closet that still held clothes. After dragging my multifunctional ladder into the little closet, I started to remove the panel.

Opening these shadowy areas always leaves me a little surprised by what I discover. I met an inspector at recurrent training who told me he opened an attic panel and a nest of snakes fell on his head. I could never get the picture out of my head after hearing that. Abruptly, the panel rose, and I pointed my spotlight inside. insulation and darkness. When I positioned the panel off to the left, I discovered a lightbulb on a chain. The bulb came on as I pulled it on. Praise be. Give thanks to God for little favours. A children's swimming pool, perhaps six feet in diameter and eighteen inches high, was directly in front of me. Under the roof, I got as tall as I could and aimed my spotlight inside the plastic. There was six inches or so of murky, mould-filled water. Subsequently, I observed that the PVC pipe was leaving the pool and heading towards the soffit vent. Right on! I considered the filthy drops that were still matting my hair. Ack. I then focused my light on the inside of the roof.

I saw that there was a missing flashing near the chimney, which was letting water leak into the pool. How witty. I made my way to the back of the pool, being cautious to stay on the beams to avoid falling into the room below. Again, I figured no one would believe the arrangement unless they saw it, so I started taking photos. It's a good method to prevent a roof leak from getting inside your house, but I wouldn't suggest it.

The Test

Try this house inspection quiz if you want to push yourself and have some fun. At the end are the answers. 1. When building a bespoke home, builders go to tremendous lengths to ensure everything is perfect. This implies: At the conclusion of the build, A. the municipal code inspector may conduct an independent inspection; B. the majority of builders will not permit independent inspections. C. To check for flaws, builders already employ an inspector. D. If you want to find mistakes and save money, custom homes require many independent inspections. 2. An inspector will ensure that the house is free of termites by:

A. Tap the walls gently at different intervals to detect acoustical sound variations.

B. Remove a minimum of one baseboard from each room to inspect it for termites.

C. Suggest that the customer use a certified pest control expert to check the house for termites.

D. Take the insulation off of attic spaces to find pests.

3. One feature of radon gas is that it ascends to the top floor of a building and is lighter than air. A property with high levels of radon will always have it, and lowering the amount C is difficult. The cost of a radon D test is high. It is nearly always easy to reduce radon levels to safe levels if an inspector tests and detects high levels.

4. The most common places for structural flaws to be discovered by inspectors are: A. the decks; B. the roof; C. the foundation; D. the attic 5. A buyer's house inspector could become irate if they are required to conduct an independent inspection; B. The buyer and

buyer's agent wish to attend the inspection; C. The seller and seller's agent want to attend the inspection; D. If the buyer is unable to attend but the buyer's agent can 6. Those that inspect homes are: A. experts; B. ex-code enforcement officers; C. additionally, home appraisers; D. generalists 7. Check for accreditation from a national association before hiring a house inspector. Examples of these associations are the American Society of House Inspectors (ASHI), the Real Estate Board of Inspectors (REBI), the American Association of Code Enforcement (AACE), and the National Association of Builders (NAB). 8. Following your home inspection, the inspector will: A. Determine the necessary repairs and estimate the cost; B. Send the seller a letter outlining the repairs; and C. Rate the home's quality on a scale of A to D. D. Compose a thorough report that will be sent to the individual covering the expense. 9. Select an inspector who possesses the following credentials: A. recent certification B. extensive experience C. real estate licence D. appraisal licence 10. The following people can benefit greatly from a house inspection report: A. Seller; B. Owner; C. Custom home builder; D. All of the above Answers are on the following page.

ANSWERS: 1. D. If you wish to identify mistakes and cut costs, custom residences require multiple independent inspections. I would have at least four house inspections for bespoke homes. A flat price that is about twice the cost of a standalone examination will be charged to you. Inspectors enjoy performing these, and if you ask for one, they'll typically give you a discount. 2. C. Suggest that the customer use a certified pest control expert to check the house for termites. There's no scientific way to assess termite damage with wall tapping, and inspectors won't pull anything apart. 3. D. It is nearly always easy to reduce radon levels to safe levels if an inspector tests and detects high levels.

Installing a foundation vent or caulking foundation cracks can effectively mitigate radon. There are also active ventilation devices that can significantly lower radon levels. 4. A. The cards. I have inspected decks, and seventy percent of them have some sort of structural flaw. The deck is often held to the house by its attachment—or lack thereof—to the ledger board or by the absence of structural beams and deck supports. 5. A. The seller desires to be present for the inspection, as does the seller's representative. Since they are the ones employing the inspector, it is customary for the buyer and/or buyer's agent to be present during the inspection. Should the seller and the seller's representative appear, it can lead to an embarrassing scenario where questions are raised by all. D. All Purposes. A high-level evaluation of all the systems and components is the hallmark of a good inspection, regardless of the credentials and backgrounds of the inspectors. The seventh is the American Society of Home Inspectors (ASHI). Some exist, most notably InterNACHI, the International Association of Certified Home Inspectors.

Currently, over 35 states mandate ongoing education and licensing. 8. D. Compose a comprehensive report that will be sent to the buyer. Both you and the inspector own the report for which you are paying the inspector. It is not necessary for you to provide it to anyone else. 9. B. Numerous years in the field. It goes without saying that you want to employ an inspector with credentials, including association membership and, if necessary, state licensing. However, the range of knowledge that years of expertise afford an inspector makes them the most significant factor. An inspector's years of expertise also help them see home flaws objectively. Inexperienced inspectors may be fussy, unduly preoccupied with structural flaws, and fail to select the best language to characterise them. Additionally, inexperienced inspectors could make snap decisions and recommend pointless, potentially expensive specialised inspections. 10. D. Each of the preceding Whoever orders a house inspection report will find it valuable in the long run.

Regular home inspections can help owners avoid unexpected upkeep expenses. What was your performance? Give yourself an A if you answered eight questions correctly or more. Give yourself a B if you answered questions six through seven correctly, and a C if you answered questions three through five correctly. Please let me know if you answered less than three correctly so I can revise this book.

Query and Response Section

All the Information about Home Inspection You Were Afraid to Ask A House inspection: What is it? A home inspection is a process that aims to provide the customer (seller, buyer, or homeowner) with an enhanced understanding of the general state of the house by evaluating the systems and components of a home that are visible and accessible, such as the electrical, plumbing, roofing, heating and air conditioning, and construction. The person who asks for an inspection of a house they are serious about buying is usually the buyer. A house inspection can reveal significant flaws that would be costly to fix and that the seller or owner may not be aware of, providing information that allows decisions regarding the purchase to be verified or contested. It doesn't discuss the cost of repairs or provide an estimate of the property's value.

It does not ensure that the house satisfies regional building codes or shield a customer in case one of the items under inspection turns out to be defective later on. A house inspection should be viewed as an assessment of the property on the day of the inspection, taking into account typical wear and tear for the age and location of the home, rather than as a "technically exhaustive" examination. For additional costs, a home inspection can also include energy audits, pest inspections, pool inspections, radon gas testing, water testing, and several other specialised issues that could be unique to the area of the nation where the examination is conducted. In addition to homeowners looking to take care of their properties, avoid unpleasant surprises, and maintain the highest potential return on investment, sellers can employ home inspections prior to advertising their properties to discover whether there are any hidden issues.

The following are significant findings from a house inspection that should be noted: 1. Serious flaws include large differential foundation fissures, an uneven or plumb structure, improperly placed or supported decks, etc. The cost of fixing these things is high. Major items are those that need repairs costing more than two percent of the original purchase price. 2. Items that could develop into significant flaws, such as a roof flashing leak that might get worse, damaged downspouts that might allow water to seep in and produce backup, or an improperly fastened support beam. 3. Dangers to safety include exposed electrical wire, bathrooms and kitchens without GFCIs, decks raised more than 30 inches above the floor without safety railings, etc. Your inspector will provide you with advice regarding these issues. He or she may suggest evaluation by trained or licensed experts who are experts in the defect areas; on major issues, they most likely will.

For instance, if your inspector discovers any components of the house that are out of alignment, they may advise you to contact a professional building or structural engineer as this may be a sign of a major structural issue. I take it that a buyer does a home inspection only after they sign a contract? Not every time. A house inspection can be utilised by purchasers seeking to ascertain the condition of the possible home, sellers looking to increase the sellability of their property, current homeowners using it as a maintenance tool, and interim inspections in new construction. Getting a home inspected before listing can be beneficial for sellers in particular.

Just a handful of the benefits for the vendor are as follows: The house is familiar to the seller. The history of any issues the house inspector discovers can be answered to his or her queries. When determining a reasonable asking price for the house, a home inspection will assist the seller in being more impartial. The report can be used by the seller to create a house marketing piece.

Before the house is available for viewings, the seller will be informed of any safety concerns that are discovered within. After the contract is signed, the seller can take their time making repairs rather than being hurried. For additional details on seller inspections, see Chapter 2. What makes a house inspection necessary? There are more than ten thousand parts in your new home, including HVAC, appliances, ventilation, and heating and air conditioning systems. Together, these appliances and systems provide durability, comfort, and energy savings.

However, weak points in the system might result in a variety of issues that shorten component life and cause a loss of value. Would you purchase a used automobile without having it inspected by a licensed mechanic? Your house is far more intricate, therefore having a comprehensive inspection that is recorded in a report gives you a wealth of knowledge on

which to decide upon. Do home inspectors examine apartments in condominiums? Indeed, and that's a wise move. You are in charge of your own unit's maintenance when you purchase a condo. According to my experience evaluating condos, a single living unit might encounter just as many problems as a home. Evaluating the common areas will also show how well the association is maintaining these places. You can choose between a complete inspection, which looks at the state of the common spaces as well as the interior of the unit, and a unit-only inspection.

Crawl spaces and attics that are attached directly to a unit will be inspected thoroughly. In addition, the inspector will evaluate the roof, common areas, garages, and basements. Common areas are not under your purview, but their state provides information for upcoming evaluations. Items for inspection consist of: Check the flooring and walls for water damage, warping, and cracks. Safety features and smoke alarms Water force Appliances systems powered by electricity Air Conditioning plumbing installations Doors and windows Common decks, patios, and balconies overall state of common areas It makes sense to take the time to examine not only the soundness of a specific condo unit but also the soundness of the condominium association, given the findings in buildings showing poor condition in high wear and tear places (like the Florida shore).

Is there a sufficient cash reserve for upkeep? You will discuss the material findings of the inspector with them, but it is up to you to investigate the board's condition further. A significant future assessment that will trap you financially is what you want to stay away from. Prior to choosing to purchase a condominium unit: Have the entire unit inspected. A competent inspector may be suggested by your agent. Examine the minutes of annual meetings over the past few years. Are reserves enough to cover maintenance needs in the future? According to a letter written by the president of the association prior to the collapse, the condo building that collapsed in South Florida in 2021—Champlain Towers South—needed fifteen million dollars in maintenance, but the board only had seven hundred thousand dollars in reserves.3. Examine the records that are available to the public.

Does a lawsuit about building defects exist? Violating the building code? Actions taken by enforcement? Study the bylaws of the association. This will indicate the amount of insurance you require. Your realtor can put you in touch with experts who can assist you with this research. As with a free-standing home, you should confirm that you have sufficient insurance coverage against both surprises and unanticipated events. Why am I unable to conduct the inspection myself? The majority of purchasers are not knowledgeable, skilled, or impartial enough to conduct their own home inspections. They are able to learn more about the state of the property by hiring a professional home inspection.

This includes if any objects are not working as intended, negatively impact the home's habitability, or require a specialist to look into them further. Recall that the house inspector has extensive training in all aspects of every home system and is a generalist. Why am I unable to have a handyperson or contractor in my family come look over my new house? Even though your nephew or ant might be quite talented, they lack the specific test equipment and information needed for an inspection, as well as any professional training or experience in home inspections. Training and experience in home inspections constitute a unique, regulated profession with exacting standards of practice.

When they buy a house, the majority of contractors and other trade professionals engage a qualified home inspector to evaluate their own properties. How much does it cost to check a house? Fees are determined by the home's size, age, and other features. A trained professional home inspector will typically charge less than $500 for an inspection. It is more important to focus on your inspector's qualifications than on the cost. Have they passed the NHIE exam to obtain national certification? If necessary, are they state certified? How much experience do they have in terms of years? Additionally, I would caution against hiring an inspector who has less than two years of experience because they might obsess over little issues. Refer to Inspector's Chapter 6: Selection. What is the duration of the inspection? This is dependent on the house's size and state. For every thousand square feet, you can typically budget one and a half hours.

A three-thousand-square-foot house, for instance, would require roughly three hours. It will require an additional thirty to sixty minutes if the report is also produced at your house by the business.

Does every house need to be inspected? Both yes and no. While most jurisdictions do not mandate it, I believe that a buyer who chooses not to have a home inspection is failing themselves. After moving into the house, they could experience unpleasant and expensive surprises as well as financial difficulties that could have been prevented. Must I attend the inspection? As a buyer, seller, or homeowner, it is highly recommended that you be present during the inspection. If you turn up after the inspector has finished their task, they will appreciate your care and you won't disturb them.

Refer to What Buyers Need to Know, Chapter 1. To understand what is and is not covered in the inspection, carefully read the inspection agreement. You should contact the inspector as soon as possible, ideally within 24 hours, to bring up any concerns you may have about the inspection or the report. It is possible and a good idea to arrange for the inspector to come back after the inspection to show you things. On a follow-up walkthrough, however, you might be paying for the inspector's time. Should the seller show up for the buyer's requested home inspection? Since it is their house, the seller is welcome to attend the inspection, but they should be aware that the inspector is representing the buyer. If the seller was not aware of the items being pointed out, the seller may find the exchange between the inspector and the buyer upsetting, and the seller may become extremely emotional about any problems that are discovered. For this reason, before offering the house for sale, the seller may wish to think about doing their own inspection.

Usually, agents would suggest to their seller customers not to be at the house when the inspection is taking place. The fact that this prevents embarrassing situations makes me think it's a good idea. Does a home need to pass a home inspection? No. A home's current state is examined during a home inspection. It is not a municipal inspection, which confirms conformity with local codes, nor an assessment, which establishes market worth. For this reason, a home inspector cannot pass or fail a dwelling. The inspector will provide an unbiased assessment of the physical state of the house and point out any issues that require replacement or repair. What does the inspection consist of? The list that follows is not all-inclusive. While not every inspection will include them all, the inspector will adhere to a set checklist specific to the house. Grading and site drainage Parking lot Admission Handrails and steps Decks Masonry Terrain (with reference to the house) Walls that are retained Attic, chimneys, flashings, and roofing Soffits, fascias, and eaves Walkways, patios, windows, doors, and walls Crawl spaces, basement, and foundation Operation of the garage door, floor, walls, and Appliances in the kitchen (trash compactor, microwave, disposal, range/oven/cooktop/hoods, and dishwasher) Appliances for laundry (dryer and washer) walls, floors, and ceilings Kitchen floors, cabinets, and counters Gaskets for windows and windows Hardware for interior doors Plumbing fixtures and systems entrance conductors, panels, and electrical system GFCI outlets, electrical grounding, and Fire and smoke detectors Systems of ventilation and insulation Controls and apparatus for heating Systems of distribution and ducts Hearths Controls and air conditioning Heaters and thermostats Safety features including rails, TPRV valves, and egress routes, among others.

For an additional cost, it is frequently possible to add additional items that are not covered by the basic inspection. Apart from the house inspector, several of these inspections need to be carried out by certified experts. Refer to Chapter 9, Extra Exams. If your house is located in a high-radon area, get a radon gas test. Test for Water Quality Inspection for Termites Test for Gas Line Leaks Sprinkler System Examination Examining the Spa and Swimming Pool Mould Inspection Septic System Alert System Certain specialised inspections will include your inspector collaborating with other businesses. You ought to inquire about the agreement and any additional costs. What does the inspection not cover? On inspection day, most individuals assume that everything is thoroughly inspected.

Countless homebuyers have become irate with their inspector as a result of this miscommunication. It would take roughly sixteen hours and cost you thousands of dollars to hire someone to inspect your property who is licensed in plumbing, electrical, engineering, heating and air conditioning, and other areas. Hiring a professional inspector is far more sensible because they are knowledgeable about house systems overall, know what to look for, and may, if necessary, suggest additional examination by a specialist. When inspecting your house, your inspector is also adhering to strict criteria. These can be state-specific rules or national guidelines (American Society of Home Inspectors, or InterNACHI, the International Association of Certified Home Inspectors). These carefully crafted standards are meant to safeguard the inspector as well as your house. Here are a few illustrations. We are specifically instructed not to move furniture (may damage it), turn on the water if it is off (may cause flooding), or break through a sealed attic hatch (may cause damage). Systems (like a propane tank) that were off when the inspection took place are among the things we are specifically forbidden from turning on.

The drawback to this approach is that we run the risk of missing an issue because we can't see under the furniture, operate a control, or enter the attic or crawlspace. When things are taken into consideration, though, the likelihood of missing something significant due to these regulations is rather minimal, and the recommendation regarding safety and not damaging anything within the house is sound. Ninety-five percent of inspectors believe that there are other items that should not be included in a standard inspection. These include inspecting the majority of items that are not fixed into the house, such as electronics, low-voltage lighting, space heaters, portable air conditioners, or specialty systems like alarms and water purifiers.

What if there are objects—like snow on the roof—that you are unable to examine? Unexpectedly, there are days when the weather makes a thorough home inspection difficult. The inspector will inform you that they were unable to assess the roof because of snow. The inspector will note in the report that he or she was unable to evaluate the roof, but they will be examining the attic, eves, and any other locations where they may get a sense of condition. With the snow melting, it might not be feasible to come back on a different day because inspectors are quite busy. But, you may typically pay an inspector a nominal charge to have them come back and examine the one or two issues they missed the first time around.

This is the nature of the beast. The inspector will often inspect the items again at no additional cost (beyond the re-inspection fee) if you request one. Is the inspector going to climb on the roof? If the roof is sturdy, safe, and allowable for walking on without causing harm, the inspector will proceed to walk on it. Certain types of roofs, like slate and tile, are not meant for walking on. Occasionally, the inspector won't be able to walk the roof due to bad weather, excessively steep roofs, or very high roofs. When accessibility is an issue, the inspector will utilise binoculars in addition to attempting to reach the edge. If it is feasible, they will also inspect the roof from the top windows. The inspector may learn a lot about the state of the roof just by looking at things from a ladder and the ground, and they will be able to learn much more about it from inside the attic. In this case, a drone camera comes in useful.

Drone cameras are being used by more and more inspectors to inspect roofs. Is it necessary to test for radon in my home? What is radon exactly? The answer to that is unquestionably yes in many parts of the nation. You can find a national radon map online or by asking your real estate agent about it. Colourless, odourless, and tasteless, radon is a radioactive gas that is produced when uranium naturally decays in rock, soil, and water. As radon escapes the earth, it may find its way into your house through foundational fissures and cavities. Well water can potentially be contaminated by radon gas. Second only to cigarette smoking, health regulators have found that radon gas is a severe carcinogen that can cause lung cancer. A radon measurement test, which your home inspector can conduct, is the only way to determine whether radon gas is present in your home.

Verify that the individual performing the test has received the necessary training in accordance with National Radon Safety Board (NRSB) or National Environmental Health Association (NEHA) guidelines. For further information, refer to Chapter 10: Radon Facts. How about a recently built house? Is a house inspection required? Indeed. In actuality, inspectors discover a lot more issues—some rather serious—in freshly built homes.

This isn't because your builder was careless; on the contrary, they did the best they could with subcontractors and planning; the problem is that a house has so many systems that it is nearly hard to check and fix everything before the Certificate of Occupancy (CO) is granted. To find everything that needs to be fixed, I advise having multiple professional home inspections when the house is almost finished. Refer to What Builders Need to Know, Chapter 5. It is even more crucial to have a home inspection done if the house is still new but was left unoccupied for some time prior to the sale.

It is not uncommon for me to witness major yet readily fixable issues such as disconnected vents, water, plumbing, sewage, and other lines. My house is being built. I have the builder's word that he will check everything. Should I use a third party to do recurring inspections? Yes, without a doubt. Regardless of their skill level, your builder is going to overlook stuff. Important details can and will be missed since they and the subcontractors are so focused on the house and their job. At least four interim inspections should be performed by a qualified inspector. The funds will be used wisely. What Does Pre-Inspection Entail?

Consensus? A service agreement is typically provided by service experts, and home inspections are no exception. The agreement is crucial since there is enough ambiguity surrounding the expected results of a house inspection. Some homeowners who have their homes inspected assume that after fixing the major issues, everything will be flawless.

A year later, you receive a call from a homeowner complaining that the toilet isn't flushing. Keep in mind that the inspection is merely a snapshot in time. The inspector makes it clear in the inspection agreement what is covered and what is not, as well as what you should do if you are dissatisfied with the services. You will gain a better understanding of the inspection and be pleased with the outcome if you go over this in advance. A home inspection does not ensure that all issues will be discovered or prevent problems in the future. What type of report will the inspection produce? A "report" can be found in as many different forms as there are inspection firms. It is required by guidelines that the inspector provide the customer with a written report. This might be as simple as a handwritten checklist with several press copies but no images, or it can be as complex as a 35-page professionally created report that is computer-generated and has digital pictures that can be converted to Adobe PDF for emailing and storing.

Find out from your inspector which report is used. Since the checklist is more thorough and makes it simpler for the homeowner, buyer, or seller to identify the problems with the photos, I advise using the computer-generated report. Reports in our technological age need to be emailable and online accessible to work with the majority of our devices. Beyond the abundance of information the report provides about your new house, there are several fantastic uses for it. Get estimates and quotations from many contractors, or use the report as a checklist and guide to help the contractor perform repairs and improvements. To preserve the property in excellent condition, use the inspector's suggestions and the estimated remaining life of the components in the report as a budgeting tool. In order to increase the worth of your house and impress potential buyers, if you are the seller, use the report to make repairs and enhancements. After that, conduct another inspection, and utilise this second report to help potential customers with your marketing.

Utilise the report as a starting point for continuing maintenance and as a punch list for a follow-up inspection. Refer to How to Use the Report, Chapter 8. Is it possible to email the report or download it as an Adobe PDF file? Indeed. The better, the more computerised and easily available. Are reports from home inspections available to the public? Reports from home inspections are not available to the public. The client who hired the home inspector and made the payment for the inspection is the owner of the confidential report. A copy of the home inspection report is available for the customer to share with or keep private. How can I know whether the inspector overlooked something? Since inspectors are human, mistakes do happen. To lessen the likelihood that they will overlook something, they frequently employ sophisticated instruments and methods. This comprises thorough checklists, computer-based lists, reference manuals, and a rigorous "always-done-the-same-way" approach to physically organising your house. This is among the reasons why an inspector may overlook something when they are distracted.

Should this occur, the inspector will have a predetermined method for continuing the examination. If something is ultimately overlooked, give the inspector a call to talk about it. The inspector should come back to look at what you discovered. Recall that the inspector is attempting to do the best job they can and most likely did not overlook the item due to carelessness or a lack of diligence in their technique. When I worked as an inspector, if a client requested, I would always come back to look at things for free. Will the inspector search for Chinese drywall, lead, and asbestos? Certain properties constructed before 1978 contain asbestos and lead. Most of these houses have already undergone remediation. Seek guidance from your inspector if you have any concerns. They are able to recommend an expert to you.

Between 2001 and 2008, Chinese drywall was put in the United States; the majority of the impacted residences were constructed between 2006 and 2007. Most of these houses have already undergone extensive remediation. At the time, Chinese drywall was manufactured with impurities and had a strong sulphurous odour. Seek guidance from your inspector if you have any concerns. What happens if the inspector advises me to have a licensed contractor, professional engineer, or plumber come look at something they discovered? It seems like "passing the buck" to me. Although you might be unhappy that more research is needed, your inspector is acting appropriately. The inspector is a generalist, not an expert, and the goal of the examination is to find flaws that compromise the home's functionality and your safety.

Only contractors licensed in their particular field are allowed to work on these systems and regions, as mandated by the inspection code of ethics and federal, state, and local regulations. If they inform you that a specialist is required, there can be a more serious problem that you should be aware of. You may be in for some unpleasant and costly surprises if you move into the house without having these areas inspected by an experienced professional. When the inspector does suggest additional testing, they are genuinely concerned about safeguarding you and your investment since they don't want to add to your costs or concerns. Does the inspector offer a warranty for the things they have examined? When it comes to inspected objects, most inspectors don't offer warranties to homeowners.

Recall that a house inspection is merely a visual assessment conducted on a certain day, and the inspector has no control over potential problems that might surface later. On the other hand, a few inspectors currently provide a sixty- or ninety-day service warranty on the examined products, provided by one of the US home warranty firms. This is a good deal, and for a comparatively small fee, the arrangement can be extended beyond the first term. You can go online and discover a warranty that fits your budget if your inspector does not provide one from one of the big providers. They are regenerative every year. Verify the type of coverage you will receive and whether there will be a co-pay for repairs. A house warranty is a service agreement that covers the cost of replacing or repairing covered goods, such as major kitchen appliances and plumbing, electrical, heating, and air conditioning systems. It is not an insurance policy. Roofs, windows, doors, and other structural components are not covered by these guarantees. Do the majority of inspection businesses provide money-back guarantees?

The majority of inspection companies don't advertise or provide a satisfaction guarantee. Of course, a satisfaction guarantee is a sign of excellent customer service, and it's always a plus if your inspection firm offers extra services at no extra cost. Usually, the best way to let your inspection business know you're not happy is to give them a call immediately after the inspection. You should initially speak with your inspector if you're dissatisfied with the services. Usually, they will go above and above to win your approval, even if it means coming back to the house to investigate. Give it to them now. I did provide a 100% money-back guarantee to clients when I owned my own inspection business, but fewer than 5% of clients requested it. The handful that did inquire were misinformed about what I was looking for; they believed, for instance, that the inspection included termites. It was my fault for not giving a clear enough explanation. What happens if my report reveals that the house is in good condition? Must I request a refund of my money? No, you just got some fantastic news, so don't ask for your money back. You may now close on your house purchase knowing that the property and all of its systems and equipment are in good shape.

The inspector's report will provide you with important details regarding your new house, which you should save for future use. Above all, you can be sure that you are making an informed choice about what to buy. What happens if major flaws are found during the inspection? Give yourself a pat on the back for getting an inspection if it turns out that the house has major problems (I consider a serious fault as something that will cost more than 2 percent of the purchase price to correct). You have just made a huge financial savings. Of course, learning that your well investigated home is now a problem home is disheartening, even heartbreaking, but at least you now have the information and can decide whether to work things out with the seller or move on. Maybe you'll desire the house so bad that settling on a lower price and doing the repairs yourself will be worthwhile. But just picture what would have happened if you hadn't received the inspection—some extremely terrible discoveries.

Is it possible for my house inspector to do the repairs? It is a conflict of interest for the person who examined your home to also fix it, therefore even though you can, a moral inspector will politely decline. It's a good regulation that inspectors are expressly prohibited from doing this by licensing authorities; they have to be totally objective when they examine your house. This is one of the reasons you should hire a professional home inspector rather than a contractor to look over your house; even though the contractor is technically competent and well-meaning, they will probably want to make the repairs, so you won't get an impartial assessment from them. Are the repairs the Seller's responsibility? The seller is not required by the inspection report results to make all of the repairs specified in the report. The buyer might work with their realtor to request concessions from the seller after the condition of the home is understood. There might be a price reduction, or the issue with the residence might be fixed.

What is a repair and what is a discretionary enhancement will be made apparent in the report. The parties should negotiate this matter. It's crucial to understand that the inspector is not authorised to participate in this conversation because it falls outside of their purview. Can I hire the inspector again to come check the house again to make sure everything was rectified after the home inspection and after discussing the repairs with the seller? Of course you can, and it's a wise move. The inspector will come back for a charge to check on the completion and accuracy of the repairs. What happens if, after moving into my new house, I discover issues? There is no assurance that issues found during a home inspection won't surface after you move in. Calling the inspector should be your first course of action, though, if you think that a problem was apparent during the inspection and ought to have been noted in the report.

He or she wants you to call if you think there may be an issue, but otherwise, they'll be okay with it. The inspector will visit your house to look at it if the problem cannot be handled over the phone, and they shouldn't charge you for this assessment. Their desire is for you to be happy, and they will stop at nothing to make that happen. Performing a final walk through on closing day and using the inspection report and a walkthrough checklist to ensure everything is as it should be is one approach to safeguard yourself between the inspection and move-in. In what ways has house inspection evolved over the past 20 years? The tools have significantly improved, but the principles are still the same.

The roof would always be walked by inspectors. When they can't see properly, they might use a drone camera in places they can't see clearly. Robot cameras are now able to be used by inspectors to access areas they deem unsafe. Crawl spaces and attics are included in this. In order to find concealed moisture and other issues, some inspectors now use tiny cameras and advanced infrared detection.

How To Promote & Sell Your Brand

AMERICAN First Lady Melania Trump was dressed in an olive-drab anorak from Spanish fast-fashion brand Zara when she visited immigrant children in a Texas detention centre in 2018. The words "I REALLY DON'T CARE, DO U?" were written in white, almost like graffiti, on the back of the garment. Commentators claimed Mrs. Trump's jacket revealed her true feelings for the children incarcerated. or her public responsibilities. or her union. Her spokesman asserted that there was no hidden message, despite her husband's tweet expressing her opinion of "the Fake News Media." In a way, she was correct. The message was very evident. Furthermore, it's a terrible mirror of modern life.

The jacket was practically the most existential item of clothing ever created, manufactured, marketed, and worn. Globally, Zara stands as the biggest fashion brand. It generated around 450 million pieces in 2018. The company's parent, Inditex, located in Spain, recorded sales of €25.34 billion, or $28.63 billion, for 2017. Of those sales, Zara accounted for over two thirds, or $18.8 billion. The jacket, which cost $39 at retail, was part of the company's Spring-Summer 2016 line. Production is outsourced to privately owned factories in underdeveloped nations, where there is little to no control for labour and safety, and wages are typically at or below the poverty line, in order to sell garments at a low cost and still make a healthy profit. Amancio Ortega, the octogenarian co-founder and former chairman of Inditex, was the second richest person in the world (behind Bill Gates) with a net worth of $67 billion at the time workers were cutting and sewing Mrs. Trump's jacket.

Cotton was used to make the jacket itself. One of the most damaging crops in agriculture is cotton that is cultivated conventionally.

Growing one hectare, or two and a half acres, of the fluff requires almost one kilogram (2.2 pounds) of toxic chemicals. It was lettered and painted with colouring chemicals that would contaminate the land and groundwater when they broke down in a landfill. The item would be worn seven times on average before being thrown away. Despite the backlash directed at Mrs. Trump for wearing it during that visit, it's unlikely that she will wear it ever again. So the jacket would go to the garbage, much like most modern apparel. "I don't really give a damn, do you?* EVERY DAY when we wake up, we ask ourselves the fundamental question, "What am I going to wear?The choice is carefully considered: How do I feel? How is the weather right now? What must I accomplish? How can I express myself? To envision?

Our first and most fundamental means of communication was through clothing. They communicate our goals, our occupation, our social and economic standing, and our sense of value. They can give us confidence and sensuality. They might show how much we appreciate or don't respect tradition. When Virginia Woolf wrote in Orlando, "Vain trifles as they seem, clothes... change our view of the world and the world's view of us." I'm wearing a Bangladesh-made black cotton jersey dress with a white pointed collar and shirt cuffs as I sit here and write this. After seeing it on a Facebook advertisement, I clicked on it, and a few days later it arrived at my house. It is on-trend and aesthetically pleasing. But when I placed my order, did I really consider where it originated from? Did I stop to think about why it only cost me thirty bucks?

Was this clothing necessary for me? No. No. And no, no. I'm not by myself. Billions of people buy garments every day without giving the repercussions of such purchases a second thought, or even a pang of regret. The Center for Media Research said in 2013 that shopping was becoming "America's favourite pastime," with consumers purchasing five times as much apparel as they did in 1980. That came to sixty-eight clothes annually on average in 2018. Globally, people purchase 80 billion articles of clothing per year. And if the world population increases to 8.5 billion people by 2030, as experts predict, and GDP per capita increases by 2% in developed countries and 4% in developing economies every year in between, we will purchase 63 percent more fashion, or 102 million tons, if we don't alter our consumption patterns.

According to the Global Fashion Agenda report by the Boston Consulting Group, this sum is the "equivalent of 500 billion T-shirts." This is all intentional. On the approach to the gate in airports, you can pick up a full new wardrobe. You may get a custom outfit in Tokyo from a vending machine. Admire that Instagram outfit? Simply click to claim it as yours. Enter a fashion store and notice the profusion of offerings while the techno beats, surfaces shine, and the light is desert-sharp. A frenziedness descends. Curiously, price becomes irrelevant. You're so enthralled and overstimulated that you overlook such basics as quality. One day in Paris, over lunch, a former editor of a fashion magazine remarked, "It's like a sex shop." Or a casino in Las Vegas, I shot back. You spend carelessly, even freely, and even though you've most likely been duped, you still feel like you've won. "The original, pre-industrial definition of fashion was to make things together—a collective that is a convivial, sociable process we use to communicate with each other," said Dilys Williams, director of the Centre for Sustainable Fashion at the London College of Fashion, to me. "The expectation is to keep up with the ever-changing trends—[to] respond to the constant noise that says, 'Come buy something else.'" The manufacturing, selling, and consumption of clothing are currently defined as "an industrialised system for making money," and this is not sustainable. Not a trace. * SINCE THE MECHANICAL WEAVER WAS INVENTED NEARLY 250 YEARS AGO, THE fashion industry has been a filthy, dishonest enterprise that has abused both people and the environment in order to reap enormous riches.

At some point—even now—child labour, convict labour, and slavery have all played crucial roles in the supply chain. Occasionally, labour union pressure or legislation would make things right in society. But those noble deeds have been undermined by trade agreements, globalisation, and selfishness. At least 70% of the clothing that Americans bought was made in the US until the late 1970s. Additionally, for a large portion of the twentieth century, manufacturers and brands were required to abide by stringent national labour rules, thanks to the New Deal. However, "fast fashion," the production of stylish, low-cost clothing in massive quantities at breakneck speed in factories under contract, emerged as a new sector of the apparel industry in the late 1980s and was sold in thousands of chain stores.

Fast-fashion companies cut manufacturing costs in order to maintain low prices, and the world's poorest nations provided the lowest labour. Offshoring gained traction in the sector at the same time that globalisation took hold. Fast fashion began as a tiny segment of the industry, but its phenomenal success quickly changed the way that apparel—from luxury to athletic wear—was designed, promoted, and sold. The result was striking: in the past three decades, the fashion industry has expanded from a $500 billion, mostly domestically generated sector to a $2.4 trillion annual worldwide powerhouse. There have been wonderful repercussions. The labour force in developed economies took the brunt of this. 56.2 percent of clothing bought in the US in 1991 was produced domestically. It has decreased to 2.5 percent by 2012.

The US textile and apparel industry lost 1.2 million employment between 1990 and 2012, according to the Bureau of Labor Statistics. That amounted to over 74% of the labour force in the sector being diverted to Asia and Latin America. Across the South and along the Eastern Seaboard, once-thriving industrial hubs began to resemble ghost towns as factories stood empty and laid-off workers applied for unemployment benefits. In the 1980s, one million people in the UK worked in the textile sector; today, barely 100,000 do. The majority of western Europe experienced the same thing. This while the number of jobs in clothes and textiles nearly increased to 57.8 million globally from 34.2 million. The West experienced severe and catastrophic trade imbalances as a result of offshoring. US apparel imports came to approximately $82.6 billion in 2017, while exports came to approximately $5.7 billion. Britain imported 92.4% of its apparel in 2017. Only Italy was able to maintain its hold on the EU as the "Made in Italy" badge denotes quality and has prestige in the market for high-end clothing.

Occasionally, a controversy involving offshore would make headlines. Ralph Lauren faced criticism in the summer of 2012 after it was revealed that the US Olympic team's uniforms were manufactured in China. Senate Majority Leader Harry Reid, a Democrat from Nevada, stated that the US should "burn" them, while Forbes described it as "clearly a PR disaster." Republicans from Ohio, including Speaker of the House of Representatives John Boehner, claimed that Ralph Lauren and his executives "should have known better," yet what infuriated the lawmakers didn't deter customers—quite the opposite. They knew, as Lauren did, that money is more important than anything else.

Given the option to purchase pants made in the US for $85 or $50 made overseas, 67% of respondents to a 2016 survey stated they would choose the less expensive option. Even when the household income exceeded $100,000 annually, the same response was given. For the whole business, the fast-fashion revolution has been immensely profitable. Owners of fashion companies made up five of the fifty-five richest people in the world in 2018. excluding the three Walmart Waltons. * Human rights in underdeveloped nations have been the second casualty of the fast fashion era. Fashion is the most labour-intensive business in the world, employing one in six people worldwide—more than both agriculture and military combined. Less than 2% of them are paid a livable wage.

The majority of garment workers are female; however, some are male as well. It was discovered in 2016 that minors refugees from Syria were employed by H&M, Next, and Esprit to sew and carry packages of clothing at subcontracted workshops in Turkey. There are factories that are of such poor quality that they collapse or catch fire (the brands have allegedly remedied the matter since). Workers are compelled to look for less respectable ways to make ends meet because income is so pitifully low. "We met a female worker in Sri Lanka who was experiencing dental pain. An NGO representative addressed a standing-room audience at SOCAP17, a conference in San Francisco "dedicated to accelerating a new global market at the intersection of money and meaning," explaining that she had to take out a loan because she couldn't afford a dentist appointment on her pay. "She couldn't afford to pay back the loan, so she had to become a sex worker to make the money to pay it off," the advocate continued. Earth has been the third victim, all the while continuing to produce clothing for a major and well-known supplier that you and I wear.

The haste and avarice of fashion have completely destroyed the environment. According to World Bank estimates, the industry contributes roughly 20 percent of all industrial water pollution each year. It contributes 10% of the carbon emissions in our atmosphere; one kilogram of fabric produces twenty-three kilos of greenhouse gases. One-fourth of all chemicals generated globally is consumed by the garment sector. A single cotton T-shirt necessitates a quarter of a pound of synthetic fertilisers and 25.3 kilowatts of electricity for production. Additionally, the World Wildlife Fund (WWF) reports that the cultivation of cotton can consume as much as 2,700 litres of water. Washing synthetic fabrics, whether at home and in mills, releases microfibers into the water. Researchers at the University of California, Santa Barbara found in 2016 that as much as 40 percent find their way into rivers, lakes, and oceans, where they are consumed by fish and mollusks before making their way up the food chain to humans.

In the same year, the Global Microplastics Initiative analysed 2,000 samples of fresh and saltwater, and found that approximately 90% of them had microfibers. Greenpeace discovered microfibers in Antarctic waters in 2017. 20 percent of the more than 100 billion garments made annually are unsold—the remnants of "economies of scale"—and are typically buried, destroyed, or burned, as Burberry shamefully acknowledged in 2018. The amount of clothing that Americans discard has doubled in the past 20 years, rising from 7 million to 14 million tons. That comes to 80 pounds annually per individual. Every year, 5.8 million tons of clothing and textiles are disposed of by the European Union.

We discard 2.1 billion tons of clothing annually. With the justification that the poorest continent requires free clothing, a large portion of it is transferred to Africa. The East African Community (EAC), which is made up of Kenya, Uganda, Tanzania, Burundi, Rwanda, and South Sudan, is said to import up to $274 million worth of worn clothing annually, according to a 2017 USAID assessment. Just Kenya takes in 100,000 tonnes a year. In Nairobi's Gikomba Market, worn clothing vendors resell some of these items at steep discounts; a pair of pants, for instance, costs just $1.50.

The native clothing industry on the continent has been so severely damaged by our fashion bulimia that the EAC decided to phase out the importing of secondhand clothing in a three-year period in 2016. With the exception of Rwanda, the EAC gave in to the Trump administration's threats of a trade war in 2018, claiming that the ban would result in the loss of 40,000 jobs in the US.

The administration persisted in threatening the little nation. What about our remaining leftovers? garbage dump. According to data from the Environmental Protection Agency, 10.5 tons of textiles—mostly clothing—were disposed of in landfills by Americans in 2015. Textiles are the fastest-growing waste stream in the UK, where 9,513 garments are disposed of every five minutes (the EPA has not provided an updated figure during the Trump administration). The majority of clothing is made of synthetic materials, most of which are non-biodegradable. The materials that do decompose, like Mrs. Trump's Zara jacket, frequently include toxins that harm the water table and soil. Certain brands have retreated. The pro-environment American outdoor gear company Patagonia ran a full-page advertisement in the New York Times on Black Friday, 2011, the day after Thanksgiving and traditionally the start of the Christmas shopping season.

The advertisement featured a picture of a zip-up fleece with the copy line, "Don't Buy This Jacket," and admitted that the jacket's production "required 135 litres of water, enough to meet the daily needs (three glasses a day) of forty-five people," "generated nearly twenty pounds of carbon dioxide," and "left behind two-thirds its weight in waste." This jacket comes with an environmental cost higher than its price, the company said. (And this was before the discovery of microfibers in our waterways.) However, its true message was ignored. According to the National Retail Federation, Americans spent a record-breaking $52.4 billion in those four days, up 16% from the $45 billion spent in 2010. "I don't really give a damn, do you?* The word "polis" in ancient Greek means "city." The Greek philosopher Plato proposed in The Republic, a Socratic conversation, that the four cardinal virtues of a perfect polis should be wisdom, courage, moderation, and justice.

The Industrial Revolution and the modern clothing system originated in Manchester, an English city in the seventeenth century. If everyone coexisted peacefully, the polis would achieve complete equality—a "just city." Known for its enormous production capacity, "Cottonopolis," as it was called, was the first significant manufacturing hub in history. Tycoons controlled it, effectively enslaving battalions of labourers. One hundred years later, Fritz Lang, the German expressionist director, showed how dangerous social and economic imbalance might be in his silent film Metropolis. The science fiction masterpiece painted a picture of a dystopian future in which the poor toil in gloomy underground factories in order to support a wealthy few in gleaming skyscrapers.

While our technology has changed, our morality has not. Cottonopolis and Metropolis represented profit-driven capitalism in their respective eras. We have Manchester and Lang on a worldwide level in today's Fashionopolis. The rag trade has a sordid past, but not an entirely one. There was a time in the middle of the 20th century when the clothing industry was doing some things correctly; people knew who cut and made their garments. Their church was the same. or their children went to the same school. Alternatively, they were connected. Indeed, there were injustices. But not to the extent that they could today due to closeness, which prevented customers from being indifferent. That's not the situation anymore. We consider ourselves to be more intelligent, equitable, and compassionate than our forebears. more sophisticated. that we aren't doing any damage by buying $20 jeans and $5 t-shirts by the bag load.

We may even be providing decent work for folks in need halfway over the world. I can tell you that this is not the case because I have spoken with dozens of workers and visited numerous offshore factories. However, I have also discovered a lot of reasons to have hope during my reporting. The apparel industry is being driven to shift toward a more principled value system by the heroic efforts of fearless activists, artists, entrepreneurs, inventors, investors, and retailers, as well as the unabashed demands of a growing generation of conscious consumers. Global visionaries are reshaping the business model with hyperlocalism in rural areas such as the American South; a resurgence of (smarter) manufacturing in New York, Los Angeles, and throughout Europe; a cleaner denim process from cotton fields to finishing plants; an all-encompassing approach to luxury that will permeate the Paris runway to online resellers; technological advancements that will revolutionise the manufacturing of apparel; and a complete and swift rethinking of how we purchase clothing. The slow food and organic movements encouraged us to think more critically about the effects of alimentary industrialization and to become more knowledgeable about the foods we eat more than ten years ago.

In the case of fashion, this has not generally occurred. Still. Fashion's changemakers are working to return sourcing and production to a human scale through modern, mediated methods, much like the sustainable food movement did. Many are aiming for a vertically integrated system, which would keep everything under one roof and spare you the headaches associated with an international, opaque supply chain. The Fashionopolis of the future might be just as well, if not better.

As customers, we are essential. It's time to stop the mindless purchasing and reflect on our cultural and spiritual actions. We must comprehend how we arrived at this point in order to advocate for change. We must examine the game known as Fashionopolis. Then and only then can we improve. When we consider, "What should I wear today?We ought to be able to respond with pride and knowledge. Although we have been dressing casually, we are able to dress consciously. Time to take this seriously. At the 71st Cannes Film Festival, Cate Blanchett. George Pimentel/Getty Images, © 2018.

Prepared For Wearing

A stunning sleeveless bubble-hem gown was worn by Australian actress and jury president Cate Blanchett as she walked the red carpet on the third night of the 71st Cannes Film Festival in May 2018. The vibrant floral design on the bodice started off as paint-by-numbers black-and-white line drawings before burst into full-blown Technicolor on the voluptuous skirt. Thoughtful and intricate, it was masterfully crafted by Mary Katrantzou, a Greek-born, London-based womenswear designer that most customers have never heard of yet have probably worn. One of the creative forces behind the Fashionopolis engine is Katrantzou; her unique silhouettes, created in her little London workshop, are carried by upscale stores in major cities.

The top of the fashion pyramid is where premium fashion designers like Givenchy's artistic director Clare Waight Keller, Virgil Abloh of Louis Vuitton menswear, and Gucci's creative director Alessandro Michele sit. The massification that makes up the bottom of the fashion pyramid is exemplified by fast-fashion businesses copying and selling the clothing that Katrantzou and her colleagues design at low prices in chain stores. The hucksters who sell the fakes, known as "knockoffs," make millions of dollars doing so. Meanwhile, Katrantzou gains nothing from the unapproved worldwide release of her work: fame, cash, or recognition for starting trends or adding to the fashion dialogue. We all wear; others prosper while she toils. Seems unjust? Yes, it is. However, the fashion business operates on a trickle-down model, as Meryl Streep incisively explained in the "cerulean-blue sweater" scene from the movie The Devil Wears Prada.

It all started very simply at Première Vision Paris, a completely unglamorous semiannual trade event held outside of Paris close to Charles de Gaulle airport. Every February and September, for three days, over 60,000 professionals in the apparel trade from 120 countries converge on the multihall Villepinte convention complex to peruse the world's largest collection of leather goods, textile designs, accessories, and manufacturing innovations in one location. In February 2019, 1,900 exhibitors participated in this event. Yarns, textiles, and sourcing solutions take up one hall. There are still more fabrics—roughly 20,000 in total—to develop. There are ten thousand more leather. an addition to accessories. An army of trend-forecasting consultants, thread suppliers, colour businesses like Pantone, and exhibits showcasing the season's trends puncture the interminable rows of office-grey sales kiosks. Every major fashion brand, as well as many smaller ones, starts to develop their new season during Première Vision.

During the winter of 2018, I travelled to Première Vision, or "PV" as it is known in the fashion industry, with Raffaella Mandriota, the twenty-seven-year-old Italian metalhead who is Katrantzou's go-to fabric specialist. She chose Maison Margiela Tabi boots. She was scouting for the women's wear collection for Spring-Summer 2019, which will be unveiled on a London runway in nine months. Canepa, a renowned Italian mill and one of her frequent suppliers, was her first stop. She said hello, grabbed an espresso, and quickly browsed through endless ranks of solids, patterns, and jacquards, or "bases," giving each one a thorough look and feel to comprehend texture and pliability, even if just for a tenth of a second. She pulled and put it on her mounting pile, or "selection," on the table when she believed it might work. After she was done—no more than ten minutes—a representative of the corporation wrote up the order. Mandriota needs coffee since she completes her to-do list a lot—she performs this twelve to fifteen times a day at PV.

A broad range of styles were on display, including orange devoré on black chiffon, kelly-green viscose, white polyester waffle-weave, grey silk inkjet-printed with a cloudy sky, and navy, black, and evergreen Fortuny-style pleated silk with green and blue coral motif. Trends were evident, including natural dyes, seersucker, colours reminiscent of Candy Land, Lurex, hemp, and iridescent silks. "This one is gorgeous," she remarked, placing the coral swatch on her stack. "Mary has a thing for pleats." Mandriota kept a close eye on her spending. She informed me that the cost of Chinese silk had increased by 20% alone this season. China is exporting less because of rising domestic consumption. And the silkworm cocoons are dying as a result of pollution." Mandriota asked her vendors a lot of questions during her search, like, "What's the minimum order?"Is there anything sustainable or organic?What more hues are offered?Is printing possible on this?"Is it possible to emboss wool?Could you use the same jacquard approach to interpret Mary's design?I think she requested a thousand or more samples during our two ten-hour days at Première Vision.

After six weeks, Katrantzou's prewar loft in Islington started receiving containers with samples. She went through edit after edit with her helpers, reducing the bulk of material to a workable assortment that might tell the story of the season. Born in 1983 in Athens, Katrantzou is a stunning woman with mink-like eyes and hair that falls straight to her elbows. Her grandfather founded Katrantzou Spor, the largest department store in the city until it was destroyed by fire during the political unrest in Greece in the 1970s. Her mother owned a furniture business and an interior design shop, while her father worked in security. Katrantzou travelled to Providence, Rhode Island, in 2003 to study interior architecture at the Rhode Island School of Design.

She went to Central Saint Martins College of Art and Design in London as an exchange student halfway through her sophomore year to study textile design for interiors. She told me, "I loved the idea that textiles were about the surface. There was an immediacy about it that I hadn't found in architecture." Adrift, she continued her studies, earning a master's in fashion with a concentration in prints and a bachelor's in textile design at a time when the more artisanal silk screen method—in which a piece of mesh cloth (originally silk) is etched with an image, stretched over a wood frame, and squeegeed with ink—was giving way to digital fashion printmaking, which is computer drawn and generated. Her signature technique of magnifying common objects in print on fabric has subsequently become her leitmotif. She sent out 10 identically shaped dresses printed with a trompe l'oeil of enormous jewellery for her MA degree show in February 2008.

She launched her own line during London Fashion Week the following September with funding from the British Fashion Council's NEWGEN emerging talent fund. She was picked up by several major retailers, including Browns in London, Joyce in Hong Kong, and Colette in Paris. She was the 2011 British Fashion Awards Emerging Talent winner in the women's wear category. She has fulfilled her promise to such an extent that, in the beginning of 2018, she sold a portion of her business to Yu Holdings, a start-up fund based in Hong Kong that is directed by Wendy Yu, a driven 27-year-old Chinese investor in technology and design. (A few weeks later, Yu also revealed that her company was funding the post of chief curator at the Costume Institute of the Metropolitan Museum of Art.) Yu designated a $20 million infusion for Katrantzou, funds that will support the expansion of the brand. "Within the next ten to twenty years, Mary has the potential to become a worldwide lifestyle brand," Yu stated. Katrantzou determined that the new collection, which would commemorate her tenth anniversary, should be a best-of, reinterpreting her previous print patterns and silhouettes in a more contemporary and sophisticated manner.

She selected vintage postage stamps, blown-glass perfume bottles, nature—including insects, butterflies, and seashells—and the arts as her topics. Mandriota requested that a few textile producers recreate the jacquard samples she had chosen at PV in the new print patterns by Katrantzou. Katrantzou, Mandriota, and women's wear expert Gregory Amore met at a wooden IKEA table at the beginning of May to discuss the updated versions. It had been suggested that one jacquard, a quilt-like brocade from the Italian mill Ostinelli Seta, would make chrysanthemums in a gritty blue colour scheme. The fabric and technique were retained by Katrantzou, but she replaced the flowers with a collage she made.

The collage featured burnt orange, Mediterranean azure, antique gold, and iridescent white as the primary colour scheme, and it featured piles of gems, ornaments, and ropes of pearls that looked like they belonged in a pirate's treasure chest scattered across a coral seabed. To observe how the varied offers took the colour, Katrantzou had stretch cotton poplin fragments, purchased from different firms, custom dyed, or "lab dipped," in the Pantone hues she chose: sandy beige, Tiffany blue, and sunshine yellow. The first test didn't impress her much since the tones seemed a little flat, like they had been rinsed in murky dishwater. Another she warmed to right away—from a different supplier. The quality of the cloth was obviously better, and the colours were more accurate. Feeling one of the swatches, she commented, "Everything about this feels lighter, and somehow thicker." "It feels more substantial," Mandriota remarked. "It's more precious." "However, the cost is doubled," Katrantzou remarked. "Yes." After receiving the final fabric selections from the mills, Katrantzou selected a few panels and had them embroidered in Mumbai. (She relies on three small family-owned workshops in the UK, two in Italy, and one in Portugal for short runs of twenty to fifty pieces.) Garment samples were made, either by her in-house atelier or a contracted factory.

India is a centre for handcrafted fashion embellishments. She worked as a house model for six weeks, fitting her longtime Swedish blonde Julia. Katrantzou remarked, "Julia has an opinion on the aesthetic." In late June, Katrantzou showed retailers her completed "precollection," which is more commercial in nature, in a Paris showroom she rented during menswear week. "She understands the fit, and advises us," Katrantzou said. It was a beautifully belle epoque Parisian space, a one-floor walk-up with patinated oak panelling, herringbone parquet flooring, and arched windows with a view of the Place des Victoires (buyers hit men's shows and women's pre collections on the same trip). The completed garments were eye-catching and vibrant when they were displayed casually on models and hung on racks. Retail buyers carefully considered every item before placing their orders at little tables over coffee and petit fours. Katrantzou took a seat next to them and heard their thoughts and insights. She occasionally modifies her designs to take their advice into account. Katrantzou saved the most eye-catching and photogenic items for her "show collection," which she unveiled during London Fashion Week in September.

This is the kind of stuff that Blanchett wore at Cannes. Retailers, editors, bloggers, and reporters flocked to the Roundhouse, a rock performance venue in north London, at eight on a Saturday night, for the event. Gradually, the thirty-five models appeared one by one on the circular runway, walking to an ethereal soundtrack that Katrantzou had commissioned from her fellow Greek and friend, Oscar-winning electro-jazz composer Vangelis. A few materials that Mandriota had chosen from PV caught my eye as they passed: the organza base for voluminous day dresses, printed with the stamp motif; a delicate transparent plastic that Mandriota had pleated in Japan and layered over geometric shifts; and a romantic trapeze midi embroidered with cascading wildflowers.

As Katrantzou skipped down the runway and made her bow, the audience applauded, and the critics showered her with accolades the following morning. Before any of those reviews were published, Katrantzou's show guests posted pictures and video clips of the looks on social media, often live. Vogue.com called the collection "a walking wunderkammer of a collection," the New York Times called it "opulent mosaics of print and polygons," and Women's Wear Daily called it "fun," especially the "fantastic pieces" like the "shimmery floor-length gown with a perfume bottle picked out in sequins down the front" and "flowing nylon dresses... printed with famous works of art." Fast-fashion brands' design teams had viewed those photos, taken note of the quantity of "likes" (an instantaneous and free market study), and selected which designs they would appropriate, rework in a loose way, and manufacture abroad for pennies on the dollar each.

(One of the top online retail executives said to me as I was leaving the exhibition, 'I bet Topshop is already working on that butterfly print.') Katrantzou's designs would set worldwide trends, but she would not be involved or have any voice in the process. According to Katrantzou, "it takes three months to produce the forty prints we develop each season." And all it takes to steal them from her is a single click on a smartphone camera. Naturally, that harms her business. However, because digital print copying has gotten so simple, it also hurts "the entire collective of designers working with digital print," according to her. She is fully aware that there won't be as much original art or fresh ideas the moment we cease defending artists and their creations, whether they be in the form of words, photographs, or designs. The imitation Katrantzous would be produced in cheap fabric in a matter of weeks by underpaid labourers operating in a disjointed worldwide supply chain, and they would show up in stores selling for less than $100—a tenth, or less, of the price of the far more elaborate and opulent originals.

All those clothes would be used for a short time and then discarded. Anything that was left on the rack for longer than a week or two would be marked down, and then marked down some more, to as low as $3.99, making everything look even more dingy and lifeless with each rejecting whisk of the hanger. The management would eventually remove the leftovers from service and either burn or shred them. For 250 years, the fashion industry has operated on a massive scale through creative theft, disregard for others, corruption, and pollution. ever since a businessman from England concluded that speed was superior. * Richard Arkwright was not particularly likeable. Trained as a barber and wig maker, he was conceited, adamant, and all around unpleasant.

Scottish historian Thomas Carlyle described Arkwright in 1839 as "a plain almost gross, bag-cheeked, pot bellied Lancashire man, with an air of painful reflection, yet also copious free digestion." Worse, Arkwright had a habit of stealing, improving, and profiting from other people's inventions, such as Lewis Paul's carding machine and James Hargreaves' spinning jenny. (A number of his parents were subsequently contested in court.) In 1771, he assembled a number of these innovative devices and established the first water-powered textile mill in history in Cromford, Derbyshire. With it, Arkwright began the Industrial Revolution, which saw a shift from handicrafts to manufactured goods and gave rise to the factory system that is still in place today. The five-story building shook as the machines roared, sending cotton filaments floating through the air like a mist of snow.

The mills only paused for an hour each day, and the workers worked thirteen-hour shifts with only two brief breaks for meals. On the grounds of the plant, workers resided in brick row homes designed by Arkwright and attended a church also designed by Arkwright. There were two hundred employees at start, and a thousand within ten years. Between 1770 and 1778, "complete change had been effected in the spinning of yarns... Wool had disappeared altogether... Cotton had become the universal material," noted William Radcliffe, the owner of a nearby textile factory. By 1790, Arkwright owned nearly two hundred mills nationwide, and Manchester had gained the moniker "Cottonopolis." In 1810, a well-known Boston businessman named Francis Cabot Lowell left for Europe, supposedly in search of a cure for his health. He was really there to take advantage of Arkwright's system. In one of the most impressive pieces of industrial espionage in history, Lowell visited the mills in Manchester, learned the mechanics of the power looms, went back to Massachusetts, and rebuilt the machinery.

Three years later, he established the Boston Manufacturing Company to spin and weave American cotton that was collected by slaves on the Charles River in Waltham, which is located just west of the city. The production of ready-made clothing increased when the lockstitch sewing machine was invented in the 1830s. However, demand was still low—many people continued to make their own clothing. Then the American Civil War started. Run up quickly on those fancy sewing machines, both the Union and Confederate troops suddenly needed durable uniforms in regular sizes, meaning ready-to-wear. To accommodate the demand, factories grew or opened new locations. After the war, the soldiers looked for street clothes fashioned in the same way since they enjoyed the comfort and fit of their regiments so much. In response, producers began mass-producing menswear and later womenswear. It was the birthplace of the US clothing industry. Early American garment manufacturing was neatly split into two categories: high-end, fashionable clothing known as "fashion," which was cut and sewn in smaller batches in workshops on New York City's Lower East Side, and less sophisticated items like work clothes and undergarments, which were produced in large, standardised runs at big factories in Massachusetts and Pennsylvania.

What makes New York special? It was the busiest port in America, bringing in European wool and silks; it was also the financial hub of the country, attracting financiers keen to invest in the rapidly expanding garment industry; and it was the main immigration hub, with thousands of Europeans arriving every week in search of employment. Many were Jews from Russia, Hungary, and modern-day Poland, where embroidery was a highly esteemed craft. During the late 1800s, the garment industry employed over half of the Lower East Side's workforce, with three-quarters of those workers being Jewish. The majority of their creations were either directly inspired by or duplicated from the Paris fashion houses' displays. The most significant was Worth, which was founded in the 1850s on rue de la Paix by English immigrant Charles Frederick Worth, who is widely recognized as the founder of contemporary couture. Before Worth entered the picture, ladies would see their couturiers and order garments made to their exact specifications.

By creating "collections" of styles, which he showed to his clientele, including the powerful tastemaker Empress Eugénie, Worth overturned that system. After that, he received orders and made each gown according to size. He gave us the bustle; his silhouettes made an appearance in fashion journals and established trends. Worth established the fashion design trickle-down system that Katrantzou currently works under. Manufacturing moved northward, to trendy new steel-framed loft buildings in midtown Manhattan, as the garment business in New York City flourished. The newly completed

Pennsylvania Station was smack dab in the midst of the Garment District, as the district came to be called, which ran from Thirtieth Street to Forty-Second Street and from Fifth Avenue to Tenth Avenue, making it convenient for out-of-town retailers to visit showrooms.

The New York Garment District had more garment manufacturers than any other place in the world in 1931 due to the rapid movement of businesses. American retailing grew rapidly during the 1930s, with the exception of a temporary downturn early in the Depression. Six decades later, New York designer Bill Blass recalls, "Everyone dressed up." He wasn't exaggerating; it was a much more formal era in which neither men nor women could fathom leaving the house without the appropriate headgear. They shopped at grand department stores like Macy's and Bergdorf Goodman in New York, Neiman Marcus in Dallas, Selfridges & Co. and Harrods in London, the Galeries Lafayette and Le Bon Marché in Paris, and specialty shops like Hattie Carnegie at 42 East Forty-Ninth Street. "Some women spend all day in fitting rooms; you put on clothes for lunch, clothes for cocktails, clothes for dinner, whereas today you go to work, lunch, and dinner in the same goddam black pants suit." Miss Carnegie was perceptive.

She offered Paris originals and her own replicas of those Paris designs, which ranged in price from $79.50 to $300, in her townhouse boutique. The New Yorker magazine published an article in 1941 describing "straight, skinny sheaths with full peplums" and "black sheaths caught behind, just below the knees, with pink roses." Miss Carnegie also had an in-house collection called Spectator Sports, created in suburban Mount Vernon, with dresses priced at a reasonable $16.50 per. Joan Crawford would simply wire, saying, "Send me something I'd like." Blass, a wide-eyed seventeen-year-old from Fort Wayne, Indiana, arrived in Manhattan in 1939. "Back then, strolling up and down Fifth Avenue on Thursday evenings, when department stores unveiled their new windows, was an equally exciting experience as the thrill of an expensive Broadway opening," he said. "You began at Altman's on Thirty-Fourth Street and made your way to Bergdorf's on Fifty-Seventh Street, stopping along the way to visit Hattie Carnegie on East Forty-Ninth Street.

The window designers competed with each other in terms of outrageousness and inventiveness. The windows were all toned down during World War II, and plumed sheaths were eliminated. Bonwit Teller even employed well-known painters like Dalí to design the windows. Factories focused on uniforms and other wartime requirements. "We wore suits," ardent fashionista Olivia de Havilland once told me. "You married in a suit." However, American apparel production resurrected with vigour during the postwar economic boom. The Garment District alone employed 200,000 people in the women's wear industry, producing 66 percent of all clothing made in the country. By the end of the 1950s, jobs in Manhattan's apparel manufacturing industry were moving upstate, to Rochester, Pennsylvania, Chicago, and the Bronx, Queens, and Brooklyn; Blass was one of them, "expected," he said, "to keep [his] head down," and "be grateful that [he] had been given the chance to design $79 copies of Dior dresses." It was effectively an example of domestic offshoring. The financial rationale was that producing a dress in New York City was 17% more expensive than in neighbouring northern Pennsylvania because of rising labour and real estate expenses.

The effect was felt by the garment workers in Manhattan, whose earnings fell by 20% between 1947 and 1956. Businesses that kept their primary offices in the Garment District underwent significant transformations in their operational strategies. Fabric was cut in workrooms in Manhattan and then transported to manufacturers located outside the city, where it was sewn into garments. After that, the completed goods were transported to city warehouses and showrooms in Midtown, where they were sold to shops. Transportation was made easier by President Dwight D. Eisenhower's recently established interstate highway system. However, the plan was absurdly intricate—all in an attempt to save money. Still, it endured, and it marked the beginning of the completely disjointed global supply chain of today. The process of creating clothing started to move out of the Garment District and was replaced by something much more artistic: fashion design. The Garment District saw a surge in activity when Blass and his colleagues set up studios on or around Seventh Avenue and used nearby factories to make their works. Racks of finished clothing were wheeled down city sidewalks by Midtown labourers to the shipping terminals and showrooms. There were 400,000 workers there in 1973, which was twice as many as the 1950s high.

Needing greater space, the garment manufacturing industry in New York moved back downtown to Chinatown, where labour costs were much lower and labourers (now immigrants from Hong Kong, with both managerial and sewing abilities) were more readily available. On the Lower East Side, there were 35 Chinese-owned workshops in 1965; by 1980, there were 430 of them, employing almost 20,000 people. All told, seventy percent of the apparel that Americans purchased in 1980 was produced domestically. Everything changed when politics entered the picture. * During the beginning of his 1980 presidential campaign, Ronald Reagan proposed the North American Free Trade Agreement, or NAFTA.

Trade accords, particularly those pertaining to textile and apparel, were not new. He viewed a "North American accord," as he termed it, as a unified market "in which the peoples and commerce of its three strong countries flow more freely across their present borders than they do today." At the behest of the American cotton-farming lobby, the US government assisted in the reconstruction of the Japanese textile industry after World War II, and President Harry S. Truman enacted a trade-not-aid policy with low tariffs. The low-cost imports from Japan, South Korea, Hong Kong, Singapore, and Taiwan—the Asian "Tigers," as they were called for their robust export-driven economies—started to negatively impact the US textile sector by the late 1950s.

In response, Washington implemented complex quotas and exclusions along with increasing tariffs, a move that would last for decades beyond the Eisenhower years. Fashion executives started to outsource some work to Asia after realising that, despite the higher tariffs, it was still less expensive to manufacture abroad than it was to do it domestically. Although shipping took several weeks, turnaround time was long, but profit margins were much higher. Roughly ten percent of women's clothing sales in the US in 1960 came from overseas. Hong Kong, which specialised in cheap Western clothing, rose to become the world's top apparel exporter by the middle of the 1970s. "Never!Liz Claiborne, a womenswear designer headquartered in New York, was incensed when her business partner Jerome Chazen initially proposed offshore. "How are we going to be in charge of work being done 10,000 miles away?However, Chazen maintained that he was unable to locate adequate manufacturing capacity in the US to satisfy the rapidly increasing demand.

He had already sourced certain products in Asia when working as a buyer for Detroit's Winkleman's department store before joining Claiborne. He wondered if that would work as a remedy. Years later, in his memoir, he recalled, "My comfort level with the idea was pretty high." Clearly, Claiborne's wasn't. Thus, Chazen recommended that they test a modest order of a challenging blouse in a Taiwanese facility. "Liz was blown away when that first lot arrived by air in our offices a few weeks later," Chazen wrote. "It was far less expensive than what we had been paying, and it was nicer than anything we had done domestically." Chazen had discovered the secret to financial success: high quality and little overhead. Soon, the majority of Liz Claiborne Inc.'s clothing was being sourced in Asia, necessitating a revision to the company's production schedule.

According to Chazen, "we had to order merchandise at least six months in advance of when we could anticipate shipping the clothing to our customers." Liz Claiborne's senior vice president for manufacturing and sourcing Robert Zane recalls that in order to accomplish that, "Liz and Art would go to Hong Kong every two to three months, and they would hold court in their suite at the Peninsula Hotel," the most opulent lodging in the area. After that, the Reagan Revolution arrived, bringing with it an economic agenda heavily centred on free trade, as pledged during the campaign trail. "And they wouldn't leave until the job was done, which meant that the next season's work was designed and production was arranged." Garments transactions were often complicated.

For example, the United States let Caribbean countries to export garments to its market with unrestricted quotas, as long as the fabric was woven and cut in the country. However, they also urged firms to work with Liz Claiborne abroad. As a result, US unions became so concerned about the job flight that they were able to effectively lobby Congress to declare December 1986 as "Made in America Month." The joint resolution emphasised "the importance of buying American" and warned that the country's production capacity could be permanently reduced due to the overabundance of imports. Additionally, unions and trade associations threw themselves into "quick response" manufacturing, which would prove to be their downfall. The US Apparel Manufacturing Association created the so-called QR efficiency system in the middle of the 1980s to compete with imports from labour-intensive overseas markets.

The American apparel industry was estimated at the time to lose $25 billion annually due to inefficient business practices developed by Claiborne. These included designers conceptualising collections a year in advance, stores placing orders six to eight months ahead of delivery, and clothing being produced so far away.

Retailers made educated guesses about what may be popular, and if they were off, they were left with inventory that needed to be discounted or thrown out. In actuality, an industry that promoted new ideas was peddling outdated ones. With QR, merchants and brands would place smaller, more frequent initial purchases and only reorder when sales data showed a need, testing looks with focus groups to determine what worked before placing production orders. Reducing inventory levels, increasing inventory turnover, and avoiding cut-rate sales and leftovers were the goals. There would be less waste and losses, a leaner pipeline, and more efficient operation.

Customers could get what they wanted, when they wanted it, and where they wanted it with QR. To assist factories in implementing the plan, Kurt Salmon Associates, a management consulting firm, was enlisted. The initial investment was high—a small factory needed to invest at least $100,000. Furthermore, the system's implementation would take a year, thus the return was sluggish. In order to determine how QR would affect production if completely adopted, the Congressional Office of Technology Assessment studied the technology in 1987 under the title The U.S. Textile and Apparel Industry: A Revolution in Progress. The forecasts were uncannily accurate: instead of cotton and a sewing machine, our clothes are made by chemicals and robots.

At the time, they must have seemed like an Isaac Asimov tale. With the exception of design and equipment maintenance, manual labour has all but disappeared from the textile and clothing manufacturing process. Fibre firms, textile makers, clothes manufacturers, and merchants are connected through sophisticated communication networks, and they respond extremely instantly to market movements, making few cities referred to as "textile towns." Consumers discover a wider variety of styles and sizes available, as well as more products catered to their individual preferences. The market for textiles and fibres used in rocket ships and road building, however, might be more in demand than that for blouses and trousers. Public policy is now almost as important as traditional economic forces due to the spread of export subsidies and import protections among nations.

When a product is labelled "Made in the U.S.A.," it may not guarantee that every step of production took place within American boundaries. Small contract shops and major multinational enterprises make up the domestic industry. The mid-sized businesses that supported the sector for two centuries have essentially disappeared. Many manufacturers made the decision to use QR instead of investing in the technology. Therefore, it would take decades for the prophecy to come to pass. But enough factories adopted the new approach that it led to a surge in domestic production and a decline in imports. How long would it last, though? The topic "Could foreign competitors potentially use Quick Response concepts to once again out-compete domestic producers?" was posed menacingly in a 1990 Harvard Business School report.It was "certainly not unthinkable." In fact, fashion executive Amancio Ortega Gaona was thinking at the time of how he could adapt QR to his domestic midrange clothing company, Zara, in La Coruña, a port town in northwest Spain. Born into a family of housemaids and railroad workers, Ortega began working in the rag trade in 1949 as an errand boy for a nearby shirtmaker.

He started Confecciones Goa—his initials spelled backwards—in 1963. It was a specialty of completely unsexy housecoats. Zorba, a fashion business, was established by him and his spouse Rosalía Mera in 1975 in the upscale shopping district of La Coruña. They renamed their establishment Zara after learning that there was a café Zorba in the community. Ortega created its clothing in Spain and stuck to the traditional ready-to-wear concept, which consists of seasonal collections of stylish knockoffs. It was successful enough for him to make a solid living—by 1989, he had eighty-five stores in Spain. However, he wants more. The secret was QR. Ortega could boost sales, profits, trends, and everything else if it combined its rapid production methods with retailing. Due to the short travel times and domestic market, he was able to swiftly get clothing into stores, sell them, and replenish supplies. Seasons are obsolete; Zara consistently releases new trends onto sales floors.

Customers were drawn in by the frequent updates, and they left with more. Ortega transformed the paradigm of the clothing industry with his innovative approach, which he called "instant fashion." He started outsourcing in Morocco, across the Strait of Gibraltar, as demand grew. More labour was available at lower costs than in Spain. Furthermore, the plants remained closed, making quick delivery and simple quality control possible. Higher profit margins are the outcome. Rivals of Ortega, including Benetton, Gap, Urban Outfitters, and H&M, took note. Similar to Zara, they appropriated fashion brands' silhouettes, reworked them in less expensive materials, and sold them to middle-class customers at deep discounts. They would change the world. All of the brands accelerated sales and production to the point where they were referred to as "fast fashion" collectively. * A DECADE LATER, US President George H. W.

Bush and Canadian Prime Minister Brian Mulroney signed the Canada-United States Free Trade Agreement, marking the first step toward combining the US, Canada, and Mexico into a "common market," following Ronald Reagan's introduction of the idea. They brought in Carlos Salinas de Gortari, the president of Mexico, shortly after and renamed the agreement the North American Free Trade Agreement. The talks went on for a number of years. Most tariffs would be removed under NAFTA, advocates claimed, which would be beneficial for US businesses as the average Mexican tax on US goods was 10%. Along with creating a continental emporium with 360 million customers, it would also generate $6 trillion in economic activity annually. Consumer demand would drive American manufacturers to increase output. As he launched his campaign to obtain congressional support, President Bill Clinton emphasised in September 1993 that "NAFTA means jobs, American jobs, and good-paying American jobs." Not everybody was in agreement. Texas billionaire businessman Ross Perot claimed that NAFTA would force American industry to relocate—with "a giant sucking sound"—to Mexico in search of cheaper labour.

Perot faced off against Clinton and George H. W. Bush in his 1992 independent presidential campaign. Perot made claims that the editorial page of the New York Times considered "absurd," such as the possibility that 85 million Americans might lose their jobs. It was, of course, hyperbole. However, the central claim of his thesis was accurate: businesses did relocate overseas, including to Mexico. At least a million jobs had been lost as a result of NAFTA by 2006; some analysts put the figure significantly higher. Numerous once-virile local industries, most notably textiles and garments, had also been severely damaged. Governments persisted in negotiating trade agreements that promoted offshore despite the absence of any modifications to oversight policies or enforcement measures. China became a member of the Geneva-based World commerce Organization (WTO), an intergovernmental organisation that oversees international commerce, in 2001. The World Bank declared loudly in 2003 that by 2015, 320 million workers' earnings would surpass the $2 per day poverty line thanks to the removal of trade subsidies, tariffs, and barriers. After three years, the bank updated its estimate, stating that just 6 to 12 million people would receive the pay increase due to the offshore rush to all low-cost labour markets.

China's clothes exports to the US increased fivefold between 2003 and 2013, despite a 13.2 percent duty on clothing—nearly ten times the amount most imported goods had to pay. This demonstrated how inexpensive it was to produce fashion, as everyone from the brand owners to the supply chain could still turn a profit, even in the face of such high tariffs. What took place? the rapid growth of quick fashion worldwide. Fast fashion, like the rest of the clothing business, plodded along at a fairly good pace during the 1990s. Retail spending on apparel and accessories reached about $828 billion, or €900 billion, globally by 2000, with the US accounting for 29% of this amount, western Europe for 34%, and Asia for 23%. A significant portion of those sales were made up of fast fashion. Traditional brands would take six months to bring clothes from the drawing board to the sales floor; in 2001, Zara had 507 outlets worldwide.

In May of that year, Inditex, the company's parent, placed a 26% share on the Madrid stock exchange; Ortega kept a majority of the shares, exceeding 60%. The money from the IPO would help finance growth. With the collapse of trade barriers and the acceleration of globalisation, Zara opened approximately 1,700 new stores in 96 countries between 2001 and 2018. The stores were typically close to affluent celebrities like Louis Vuitton and Gucci in order to capitalise on their allure and attract their well-heeled clientele. During this entire period, Inditex stayed mostly out of sight. Not one interview. Not promoting anything. Not even a picture of Ortega, as there aren't many pictures of him online. His personal life is not well known; he started Inditex with his wife Rosalía, with whom he divorced in 1986; she passed away in 2013. In 2001, he wed once more.

Almost daily for ten years, one of my friends who used to write for Women's Wear Daily, called the Inditex headquarters to request an interview; each time, he was told, "Not now." However, in 2015, Imran Amed, the founder of Business of Fashion, a corporation-friendly web platform covering apparel news, and one of his reporters accepted an invitation to visit the La Coruña headquarters, which was paid for by Inditex, and published an uplifting article that ultimately revealed the inner workings of the company—as much as the powerful would permit. Amed was shocked by what he observed. "They optimise every step," he said, adding that "the scale was extraordinary and that they thought out everything from the size of the hangers to how you decide to store things." A data centre on the La Coruña campus runs around the clock to process information on the company's supply chain, sales, social media, environmental emissions, energy consumption, and more—all in an effort to cut down on time, money, and resource waste. Jesús Echevarría, Chief Communications Officer at Inditex, bowed before BoF and said, "This is where you can control the entire world." Inditex supplied fresh merchandise to its e-tailing depots and 6,500 stores twice a week.

In order to comprehend the influence of this constant cycle of refilling and updating the stock on sales, keep in mind that consumers visit the boutiques of most fast-fashion brands four times a year, whereas they visit Zara seventeen times. A style is removed from the sales floor and production orders are cancelled if it doesn't sell out in a week. If customers are drawn to it—a phenomenon that data analysts in La Coruña instantly detect—the order is repeated and produced in tiny quantities at plants in Spain, Portugal, and Morocco, all of which are close to the distribution hub. It will have run its course and be replaced by another hot new style in about a month. The reason Ortega consistently ranks in the top ten of Forbes' annual list of the world's richest people—and occasionally tops the list—is due to Zara's agile business procedures, which make the company around four times more profitable than its competitors. From 2009 to 2014, he personally made $45 billion as the largest stakeholder of Inditex. In 2018, he was still receiving $400 million in dividends, and Forbes said that he had $70 billion, making him the sixth wealthiest person in the world, behind Jeff Bezos, Bill Gates, Warren Buffett, Bernard Arnault, and Mark Zuckerberg. He had declared his retirement in 2011 and had given up full control in 2017.

Zara's sales in 2017 came close to $19 billion. Similar to earlier, its rivals opened hundreds of stores across the globe. New digital and communication technologies were applied, which further improved output, tightened manufacturing cycles, and streamlined operations. The amount of clothing manufactured doubled to 100 billion pieces a year between 2000 and 2014—or, as McKinsey analysts pointed out, fourteen new pieces of clothing for each person on the planet annually. The chain of supply broke even more. One place would be used for weaving and dyeing the fabric, another for cutting, a third for sewing, and a fourth for attaching buttons and zippers. Additionally, final details like embroidery and denim distressing were carried out in a different country. Very few fashion businesses own their factories, thus almost every stage has been outsourced or subcontracted.

Transportation via sea is preferred. Although it takes longer, the cost is far lower than by air. It's rumoured that a big fast-fashion company has outfitted cargo ships with sewing machines and other production equipment so that clothing may be created while the ship is in international seas, accelerating the process and further cutting costs. Fast-fashion retailers can lower retail prices without seeing a decline in earnings because they always seek the lowest bids. While US consumer prices increased by 50% in real terms between 2000 and 2014, apparel costs decreased during the same period. Shoppers were encouraged to buy more, more, more as stores suddenly overflowed with $5 T-shirts and $20 gowns, which were almost as expensive as Hattie Carnegie's Spectator Sports dresses during the Great Depression. Indeed, they did. People were going through clothes at a never-before-seen rate, according to McKinsey, which reported that "the number of garments purchased each year by the average consumer increased by 60 percent." "Throwaway clothes" started to seem normal. Some contend that by introducing high design to the general public, Zara and company have democratised fashion.

American Vogue editor Anna Wintour recently told me, "The more people who can have fashion, the better." However, fashion also feeds on our fears and our dwindling attention spans. Fashion images are constantly bombarding us on social media, television, billboards, and in the press, teasing and pleading with us to indulge in what one executive called a "temporary treasure." Fast fashion caters to a youthful demographic, ages eighteen to twenty-four, who tend to outgrow clothes quickly. Thirty-three percent of these consumers purchase a fashion item every two weeks, and thirteen percent do it once a week, according to research conducted by retail consultant Kurt Salmon. Eighteen to twenty-year-olds make up the younger demographic, and twenty percent of them shop online and request same-day delivery. They instantly put the item on and strike a selfie, which they then share on Snapchat or Instagram. After that, they go shopping some more and discard, donate, or resell stuff. All facets of fashion have been engulfed by this whirlwind.

French designer Jean Paul Gaultier bemoaned back in 2016 that "even designer collections are forced to adopt an industrial pace and scale... [to] compete against fast-fashion behemoths like Zara and H&M." In 2015, he gave up on ready-to-wear after forty years and dedicated all of his attention to made-to-order couture due to the hamster-wheel cycle. "Not enough people exist to warrant their purchase, hence the system is broken. We're producing clothing that will never be worn," he remarked. * Despite the saying, "too many clothes kill clothes," we continue to purchase and discard them, which encourages fast fashion to continue ripping off the concepts of other designers. Mary Katrantzou hired a lawyer in the early 2010s because she was so frustrated with the thefts committed by the Irish shop Primark.

She wasn't the only fast-fashion company to face copyright infringement lawsuits; according to a 2011 Forbes article, Forever 21 has faced about 51 lawsuits. Every case was resolved, typically for undisclosed amounts. But occasionally, financial gains have been made public, and they pale in comparison to the wealth that fast-fashion companies amass. 2011 saw Ashley Wilde, a textile designer, get $140,000 from Primark. It made more than £309 million, or about $480 million, in profit that same year. Katrantzou believed it was worth pursuing even though the payout was minimal because her main goal was to stop Primark from selling the knockoffs.

The response we received after months and months of discussion—during which they were ignoring us—was that my work wasn't genuinely cited. "I went and looked at the Brazilian designer:

he had copied me," she said. "It was referencing a Brazilian designer who I'd never heard about." A perfect replica!It appears that rapid fashion retailers imitate lesser-known copiers in order to enhance their legal protection. She went on, "This all took eight months, and in the end, Primark decided to take down everything. But by then, there was no merchandise. She sighed and gave me a saucer-eyed look. Shila Begum in Rana Plaza said, "They had sold it all." Copyright 2018, Clara Vannucci.

The Cost Of Intense Couture

I peeped through slightly ajar metal gates on the top floor of the Bendix Building, a dilapidated eleven-story Gothic Revival office tower located in the heart of Los Angeles' Fashion District, where I saw employees making clothing while crouched over machines in dimly illuminated rooms. The linoleum floor was covered in mounds of fabric; there were dust bunnies, threads, and scraps everywhere. All of a sudden, doors started slamming shut. Whoa! Whoa! Whoa! Mariela "Mar" Martinez, an organiser for the charity Garment Worker Center in Los Angeles, said, "Wow, that was quick." The neighbours had been informed by someone who had identified her. We went down to the eighth floor, where the doors to the workshop were already locked and closed.

The building was alerted. We gazed across the street at the Allied Crafts Building, another of the dissolute downtown buildings from the early 20th century housing sweatshops, at the end of the hallway. Its façade of art deco was falling apart. There were several opaque whitewashed windows. We could hear the clatter of sewing machines from a couple of the decaying sashes that were cracked apart. We strolled over after using the Bendix elevator to return to street level. A Latino man was using a pay phone at the check-cashing station in the lobby. For Martinez, the majority of L.A. The majority of sweatshop owners are Korean, and the workers are Latino. We made our way upstairs to the third floor. Window Sills were fractured. A man in his 30s, possibly a manager, was smoking while perched on one of the rusting fire escape steps. "Would you take this route?" Martinez inquired. Slender cables and antiquated wall fasteners gave the impression that it would give way under the weight of several individuals. And you'd have to hop into a Dumpster once you reached the second story, where it stopped.

As we headed back to the street, Martinez remarked, "I call this the white noise of Los Angeles." The largest centre for apparel manufacture in America is currently located in Los Angeles, despite the fact that "no one sees it, or acknowledges it." The industry had its start in the early 1900s when regional knitting mills began to specialise in swimsuits; Catalina and Cole of California were two popular brands at the time. Following World War II, it kept expanding as the "California Look," which has a casual-chic style in lighter fabrics, gained popularity all throughout the nation. The US capital of fashion production finally moved from New York to Los Angeles in the early 1990s; soaring Midtown real estate prices and NAFTA dealt a double blow to the Garment District. The California Fashion Association's president, Ilse Metchek, told me in 2017 that the local business brought in roughly $42 billion annually. Martinez calculated that 45,000 people were employed in Los Angeles to produce clothing. Of those, around half were paid at least the minimum wage in California at the time, which was $10.50 per hour.

The other half were undocumented workers making as little as $4 per hour producing clothing for US-based firms in covert factories. No extra hours worked. No advantages to health. terrible circumstances. However, the big, middle-class firms that source from these sweatshops proudly proclaim that their clothing is "Made in the USA," as if saying so instantly gives clothing made abroad greater authenticity, integrity, and quality. It's a corporate marketing ploy to exploit consumers' sense of patriotism while blatantly violating labour regulations in the United States. Sweatshops in the country have long existed. Almost all factories in Richard Arkwright's day were sweatshops. In the late 19th and early 20th centuries, the Lower East Side of New York experienced the same thing. They fled underground after being outlawed by labour laws and unions.

Domestic sweatshops, controlled by organised crime, developed into covert hubs for money laundering and people trafficking. When one is found, it occasionally hits the headlines, and the scene is almost always horrific. State and federal agents busted a covert clothing factory in Los Angeles in 1995. a suburb in El Monte that was manned by sentries and encircled by fences and barbed wire. Within, they found seventy-two Thai labourers held in slavery, $750,000 worth of currency and gold bullion, and documents demonstrating hundreds of thousands of dollars in cash transactions between banks. Domestic sweatshops have become more common due to the current pushback against globalism and the protectionist appeals to purchase American goods. This is especially true in Los Angeles, where there is a significant undocumented immigrant community.

A 2016 study co authored by Martinez and published by the UCLA Labor Center found that 72% of garment workers in Los Angeles reported that factories were filthy; 60% said that the factories' inadequate ventilation caused respiratory ailments; 47% reported that the restrooms were filthy; and 42% reported seeing rats. The brands that were purportedly produced under such circumstances included Forever 21, Wet Seal, Papaya, and Charlotte Russe, according to the research. The US Department of Labor filed charges in 2016 against these and other Southern California textile manufacturers, alleging that they had 85 percent of the time breached basic statutory safeguards like paying overtime and the minimum wage. The Department of Labor also ordered the suppliers to pay $1.3 million in back wages and damages. The majority of these suppliers were situated "right in the heart of the Fashion District—twenty blocks from City Hall," according to UCLA study coauthor Janna Shadduck-Hernández. ("Forever 21 and Russe later stated they took labour issues "very seriously"; Forever 21 added, "These entities are completely independent of Forever 21 and make independent business decisions' ').

Martinez was drawn to the fight because of this. She is a twentysomething woman who grew up in South Central, a few miles away from the Garment Worker Center. Her mother cut samples for fashion brands, and her father operated embroidery machines in the city's legal clothing sector. When she was an undergraduate at Brown University, she joined United Students Against Sweatshops (USAS), a youth movement dedicated to bringing about change through campaigns and boycotts. She also became involved in human rights activism while still in high school. She went back to Los Angeles after Brown and became an organising coordinator at the Garment Worker Center. She meets twice a week at the windowless offices of the centre, located in a dilapidated low-rise on Los Angeles Street, where she hears the complaints of the staff.

The most prevalent is "wage theft," which occurs when employers pay their employees much less than the federal or state minimum wage. She will typically get in touch with the employer directly and attempt to work out a settlement. She will get in touch with state and federal agencies, such as the US Department of Labor's Wage and Hour Division, if the matter is extremely serious. They will then begin an investigation that might lead to a raid. Martinez goes with agents on the sweeps and occasionally, she reports, she sees labels of clothing brands that advertise that their products are "sweatshop-free." When these businesses are exposed, they frequently deny knowing that their "approved" contractors are actually subcontracting to sweatshops. In the garment business, subcontracting is commonplace, resulting in a disjointed supply chain that puts workers at risk. Martinez or government representatives submit a claim for lost earnings, which is the discrepancy between the minimum wage and the amount that employees are paid.

Everybody involved in the supply chain—brands, merchants, subcontractors, and contractors—takes accountability. According to her, factories "will close shop, or reopen under a different name." "They utilise fictitious identification, or the employer may not be the one listed on the register. That will end the case. Usually, Martinez is able to recover "not even half of what's actually owed," according to her. "We will recover five thousand dollars, up to ten thousand dollars, on wage claims that total fifty thousand dollars, not including penalties. And that's when the employee has an agent. In such meetings, Martinez continued, "brands tell the contractors, 'Either you fix this or we're taking all our work away from you.' They wash their hands of the problem." Without a representative, the contractor will offer one hundred or two hundred dollars, and a lot of people take it because it's from nothing to something. Also, the contractor will not have the funds to cover unpaid wages if the brand departs. Although I don't have much sympathy for the contractors, they are merely tools in this scheme. If every garment worker in L.A.

If wage claims were to be filed, millions would be owed—millions that went straight into the CEOs' and shareholders' coffers. She gave me a gloomy expression. She remarked, "Listen, we all know our shit's made in sweatshops." Yet we pushed it to the back of our thoughts. * No one seems to care. Richard Arkwright needed cotton for his mills to succeed. A great deal of it. And there was enough of it accessible because of the extensive worldwide commerce lines of the British Empire. Cotton was the main source of income for Britain's colonies in the Americas and the Caribbean during the eighteenth century.

Grown, harvested, and loaded onto ships bound for Arkwright's industries in England were slaves. Karl Marx, a coauthor of the Communist Manifesto, subsequently noted, "There would be no cotton if there was no slavery." Modern manufacturing could not exist without cotton. Arkwright required hordes of labourers to spin the cotton. Poverty poured in from the country and towns in hundreds. Men stayed on the farm to tend to the fields; women made up the majority. Women managed households and reared children before Arkwright; he made them into wage workers. He also employed the unsupervised kids, giving them a pittance of what the grownups were paid. The Condition of the Working Class in England, written by Friedrich Engels, a German textile tycoon's son and apprentice in the Manchester cotton industry, was published in 1845 after Engels was horrified by what he saw there. He stated that mill workers were "robbed of all humanity" and kept in unspeakable destitution.

The working class in Manchester had an average life expectancy of seventeen. Half of Britain's factory workers were women; they were more affordable and submissive than men. Epidemics such as cholera, smallpox, and scarlet fever were "three times more fatal" in Liverpool than in the countryside, and alcoholism rose, with "people staggering... [and] lying in the gutter." Moreover, by the 1840s, the proportion of workers under the age of eighteen to those beyond it was equal for both boys and girls. Usually, the starting age was eight or nine. The continuous hours the Cottonopolis factory children spent on their feet slowed their growth and resulted in big, infected sores on their legs, varicose veins, and severe back discomfort. The Manchester Guardian stated that three incidents occurred in the summer of 1843 alone: a youngster was crushed to death by a cogwheel; a girl was snared by a strap and whirled fifty times around the machinery; and a lad died of lockjaw after his hand was crushed between wheels.

Unsurprisingly, young labourers attempted to flee. Some slept in storage areas, only to be discovered and physically assaulted by their superiors. Former factory child Robert Blincoe's 1832 memoir is thought to have influenced Oliver Twist because of its horrific tales. The danger to the grownups was equal. Women's pelvises were damaged by standing in twisted positions for extended periods of time, operating heavy machinery, and lifting enormous loads; this resulted in miscarriages or deaths during childbirth. Pregnancy rates soared at night while factories were in operation, and workplace rape was widespread. Workers' inhalation of fibrous dust from the plant floor caused respiratory illnesses, asthma attacks, "blood-spitting," and consumption. According to Engels, mill work constituted a new form of servitude, and some were killed by accidents like "the loss of the whole finger, half or a whole hand, an arm, etc., in the machinery."

Eventually, public protest forced the British government to enact a number of rules governing pay and working conditions in factories. Engels noted that fines were "trifling" in comparison to "the certain profits," thus the new restrictions were disregarded. What irked him the most, though, was what he perceived as the hypocrisy of England's wealthy. They praised themselves as "mighty benefactors of humanity" for their charity attempts, but in reality, these contributions only gave "plundered victims the hundredth part of what belongs to them!" the author stated. That, in his opinion, was the worst crime of them all. * Workplace abuses began in the nineteenth century when the garment industry relocated to America. Much of the altruism there was also window dressing. There were, however, certain exceptions. The Consumers' League of New York City was founded in 1890 by two young, wealthy progressives: Maud Nathan, a Sephardic Jew married to a stockbroker, and Josephine Shaw Lowell, a Civil War widow whose late husband was a nephew of Francis Cabot Lowell. The league was a nonprofit advocacy group of middle-class women committed to improving working conditions in the region's apparel industry.

Their motivation was both civic-minded and personal: they were concerned about the spread of infections from their garments, but they were also horrified by the allegations of the exploitation of female and child labour. Following that, the US House of Representatives initiated an investigation into the country's garment industry and was presented with copious evidence supporting the need for reform. However, nothing altered. Thus, campaigner Florence Kelley turned her focus to ending sweatshops in the United States. As the first general secretary of the National Consumers League, a countrywide non profit organisation that brought together local consumer organisations and was created in 1899, she made the case that the best ways to cut manufacturing costs were not via a lack of wages but rather through contemporary mechanisation and efficient distribution. She did, in fact, think that the system of sweatshops drove up costs by discouraging owners from modernising their equipment.

The National Consumers League introduced the "white label"—a garment tag that certified the manufacturer had respected state employment and safety laws as well as the League's standards—in 1899. She called for boycotts, stating: "If the people would notify [Chicago department store retailer] Marshall Field... and others that they would buy from them no clothing made in sweatshops, the evil would be stopped." The white label gave consumers more control and encouraged them to consider moral issues when making purchases. Kelley said, "We can have cheap underwear that is made ethically and clean, or we can have cheap underwear that is made inhumanely and dirty." Not Philadelphia department store tycoon John Wanamaker, though some merchants objected, saying, "Henceforth we are responsible for our choice." In addition to supporting white-label-approved clothing in his store and getting window dressers to fill the Broad Street vitrines with exhibits that highlighted the distinctions between sweatshops and white-label-approved manufacturers, he joined the League's effort to improve factory conditions.

Later, pictures from the window display travelled to trade shows across the world. Sixty American manufacturers were eligible to use the white label on their clothes in just five years. Nevertheless, a lot of industries were built on the cheap and frequently disregarded safety and health regulations. Locking emergency exits to deter staff theft was a frequent infringement.

Disasters like the Triangle Shirtwaist Factory fire in 1911 were encouraged by such circumstances. Workers on the run jumped onto the flimsy fire escape, causing it to collapse. Numerous people—many with their clothes and hair on fire—jumped out of windows and the roofs. A total of 146 workers—123 women and 23 men—passed away. Up until September 11, 2001, it was the worst workplace accident in New York City. Frances Perkins jumped in to fight back. As a forceful defender of labour rights, she succeeded Florence Kelley as executive secretary of the New York City Consumers League in 1910. Following Triangle, Perkins became a member of the factory-regulating Industrial Commission of New York State. President Franklin D. Roosevelt appointed her as secretary of labour in the 1930s, making her the first female cabinet member in American history.

The Public Works Administration, the Social Security Act, which established unemployment, welfare, and retirement benefits, and the Fair Labor Standards Act (FLSA), which established the nation's first minimum wage, guaranteed overtime payment, outlawed child labour, and instituted the forty-hour workweek, were just a few of the historic acts and agencies that were created during her twelve-year tenure—the longest in that post. The FLSA helped American industry recover and enter a new era of prosperity. aside from the Garment District. Bill Blass remembered it as "a place of Dreiserian amounts of soot and lint." "Manufacturers made every effort to create a culture of disdain... We were not allowed to use the same elevator as our bosses, even after those of us who survived the war returned home in uniform. We worked as backroom boys in the most shady company in the world—Seventh Avenue. * AND THAT'S HOW IT REMAINED, until post-NAFTA garment manufacturing shifted offshore and the majority of those workshops closed.

The old-fashioned sweatshop system sprung back into life offshore. Labour regulations were much less stringent and there was little to no control in developing economies. For this reason, the House Subcommittee on Labor Management was forced to convene hearings on worker abuses in a Honduran factory where the American womenswear brand Leslie Fay was procuring clothing within six months of Congress enacting NAFTA in 1993. In terms of American fashion, Leslie Fay had long been a standard-setter. Leslie Fay, named for his only daughter, was established in 1947 by cigar-chomping garment entrepreneur Fred Pomerantz, who had worked in Manhattan's Garment District since the age of eleven. The brand was well-known for its attractive gowns, which were stitched by union members at the Wilkes-Barre plant. By the time Fred retired in 1982, the brand had an astounding annual revenue of $500 million, was sold in 13,000 department and specialty stores across the country, and was publicly traded.

John, Fred's middle-aged son with a Wharton education who worked for decades as Leslie Fay's employee, took the company private through a leveraged buyout, a common financial manoeuvre in the 1980s economic boom. John Pomerantz made an incredible $41 million from a second leveraged buyout two years later, which was carried out by independent investors and former firm managers.

With such vast wealth, he and his spouse Laura emerged as prominent figures in the New Society, the collective term for the American super-rich of the decade. Leslie Fay returned to the stock market in 1986, and by 1990, her sales had risen to an astounding $859 million. Laura was a senior vice president and a former investment banker who was reared in a retail family. John was elected chief executive officer. While on a business trip in Toronto in January 1993, John Pomerantz received a call from Paul F. Polishan, his chief financial officer.

With foreboding, Polishan said, "We have a problem." Small, privately held clothing companies are known to manipulate accounting from season to season—counting sales orders and profits before they are actually completed and earned—in order to improve end-of-year figures. This is known as "maybe a little more than just a problem." Leslie Fay was a publicly traded company, so the figures weren't just manipulated; in reality, the company lost $13.7 million, despite reporting $24 million in revenue. Following the disclosure, the company's price plummeted, a class-action lawsuit was filed by shareholders, and Leslie Fay filed for Chapter 11 bankruptcy two months later. Pomerantz vowed he was unaware of the accounting scam, blaming it on the actions of renegade workers. Wilkes-Barre headquarters executives started a cost-cutting initiative (Polishan was later arrested and served time in prison).

Pomerantz had opposed outsourcing up to that point because he thought domestic production made more sense economically, with a quicker turnaround from plant to retail floor. He said that he believed it was morally right to continue producing things at home. All that common reason and moralising vanished with the bankruptcy. Production was relocated to Honduras by Leslie Fay, far from the management's control in northeastern Pennsylvania. It soon became clear that Leslie Fay's executives had no knowledge how the brand's clothing was created, just like so many other American apparel firms who outsource their manufacturing to other countries. They were embarrassed to hear this information from testimony at the 1994 Wilkes-Barre congressional hearings. Twenty-year-old Honduran Dorka Nohemi Diaz Lopez, a seamstress for Leslie Fay dresses and blouses, was presented to them by the National Labor Committee (NLC), a nonprofit organisation that focuses on exposing human and labour rights violations and has its headquarters in Pittsburgh. Leslie Fay's US-based workers were paid $7.80 per hour, but Lopez informed the subcommittee members that girls as young as thirteen were working on the plant floor for 40 to 50 cents per hour. Mancunian conditions prevailed in the Honduran factory.

The females worked shifts lasting twelve hours or more. There was no clean drinking water, and the temperature frequently soared above one hundred degrees. Back in Wilkes-Barre, the backlash was intense: children of laid-off workers wrote to Pomerantz, questioning him about why he took away their parents' jobs; preachers chastised the company in Sunday sermons; displaced workers organised protests; and the local papers published scathing op-eds denouncing Pomerantz for the move offshore. "The doors are locked," she testified, "and you can't get out until they let you." Jeannie Kowalewski, a fifty-six-year-old who worked as a Leslie Fay machine operator for thirty-eight years, told the subcommittee, "We always felt it was like a family." Pomerantz showed no surprise. Writing to the congressional subcommittee, he stated, "This is a nonsensical problem." The NAFTA discussion was centred around the offshoring of low-skilled jobs, and it has now concluded. * Numerous American apparel firms, such as well-known brands like Levi Strauss, J. Crew, Eddie Bauer, and Kathie Lee Gifford, were subject to comparable accusations.

As a result, companies began creating "codes of conduct," which are a set of guidelines that a business demands its suppliers to abide by. anticipates. It's not all required. Everything is optional. The necessity of standards of behaviour brought to light the biggest, and seemingly intractable, conundrum facing the fashion industry: how to manufacture goods at the lowest possible cost while maintaining respectable working conditions and wages. Prior to NAFTA, in March 1992, the executive management committee of Levi Strauss approved the first code of conduct for the fashion industry. The Sourcing Guidelines Working Group (SGWG) at Levi's, an internal task force, developed the code "to ensure the people making our products in contract factories were being treated with dignity and respect, and working under safe and healthy working conditions," according to a statement from the firm.

The SGWG took its cues from the UN's Universal Declaration of Human Rights and the International Labour Organization: no child labour or forced labour; no discrimination based on gender, race, or ethnicity; lawful working hours; equitable pay and benefits; freedom of association and collective bargaining; and sufficient environmental, health, and safety standards for all garment manufacturers. The brand's intentions were dubious. Shortly after terminating agreements with a Hong Kong-owned plant in the American territory of Saipan that was purportedly violating labour rights, Levi Strauss unveiled their code. The conditions in the plant were comparable to those in underdeveloped countries: filthy restrooms, barred fire exits, ill-maintained dormitories, and a perimeter guarded by armed guards. The businesses that used the facility to make goods, such as Liz Claiborne, Ralph Lauren, Gap, and Levi's, were permitted to use "Made in the USA" branding because the building was physically located on US territory.

The US Labor Department launched a lawsuit after finding federal health and safety violations in over a dozen Saipan-based companies owned by the same Hong Kong family, just days after Levi's implemented its policy. The owner of the plant eventually paid the workers approximately $9 million in arrears. Brands employed third-party monitors to carry out audits in order to enforce the codes. Monitors gave advance notice of their inspections, as they do to this day, so that factories could be cleaned and employees could be trained on what to say. Up to half of the factories in some nations allegedly falsified their personnel records in order to pass inspections. There was no supervision by monitors. Bribery was widespread. Scandals continued to emerge. American rappers Sean ``P-Diddy " Combs and Jay-Z were involved in a scandal in 2003 when it was discovered that the clothing for their respective hip-hop labels, Sean John and Rocawear, was produced in Honduran sweatshops. In November of that year, Lydda Eli Gonzalez, a 19-year-old Honduran garment worker, described the atrocities she had gone through at Southeast Textiles (SETISA) during a Senate Democratic Policy Committee meeting through a translator.

Sean John accounted for about 80% of SETISA's output, with Rocawear making up the remaining 20%. Towering walls encircled the industrial zone where SETISA was situated, and armed sentries stood watch at the gate, which was a closed metal structure. The office was open from 7am from 75 to 98 cents per hour, from 4:45 p.m., although unpaid overtime was required. The Sean John shirts were sold at American department stores like Bloomingdale's for forty dollars each. Every day, the factory produced over a thousand items. Gonzalez stated in court that "just one shirt would pay more than my wage for a week." Supervisors would "stand over us, calling us dirty names, like [damned] donkey, bitch, and worse, and shouting and cursing at us to go faster," she went on. The drinking water reportedly contained faeces, and the temperature increased to the point where workers were "sweating all day" due to fabric fibres and dust turning their hair "white or red or whatever the colour of the shirts we are working on." It was against the rules for employees to speak. They were searched before they could use the restroom, which they could only use once in the morning and once in the afternoon.

Usually, there was no soap or toilet paper. Pregnancy tests were administered to women; if the results were positive, the woman would lose her job. Every day when they entered the plant, they were all frisked, and everything found—even lipstick or candies—was seized. When they punched out at night, they were patted down once more. Combs quickly intervened after realising that this story could destroy his brand. The SETISA factory's production chief and deputy were fired within ten weeks, and the National Labor Committee (NLC, subsequently renamed the Institute for Global Labour and Human Rights) declared that air conditioning and a water purification system had been installed. Additionally, overtime had been made voluntary and paid. The guards had been banished and bathroom locks had been removed. Every employee would have access to public health insurance and be able to form a union. Pregnancy test abolition was also discussed. Pay, however, continued to be pitifully low. You genuinely labour only to eat. It cannot be preserved.

Nothing can be purchased. Gonzalez explained it to the Senate subcommittee as a matter of survival. "I'm in the same situation as I was two or three years ago. * IN NO PLACE is the trap more unbreakable or terrifying than in the People's Republic of Bangladesh. * We are in a trap. A narrow strip of land in the Bengal area that sits between India and Myanmar, with 168 million people living there in 2019—roughly 25% of them below the poverty level. It is the tenth most densely populated country in the world, with the ninth most people. According to the WTO, 40 million workers produced more than $30 billion worth of "ready-made garments," or RMGs, for export in the 2018 fiscal year, making Bangladesh the world's second-largest clothing producer behind China/Hong Kong. According to Siddiqur Rahman, president of the Bangladesh Garment Manufacturers and Exporters Association, "this sector accounts for eighty-three percent of our foreign currency." The garment industry employs fifty million people. It is essential to our economy.

In five years, the government intended to treble output. Bangladesh's clothing sector is relatively new, having emerged in the wake of the nation's independence struggle from Pakistan in the 1970s. At the time, South Korea had reached its limit on American textile and garment imports, therefore businesspeople in the manufacturing sector established facilities throughout Bangladesh's rural areas. Poor young women were sent to these locations by their families or flocked there in search of work, as was the case with every new location for the garment industry before it. Bangladesh became the cheapest place to create clothing—a new Manchester—with its pitiful pay and unconscionably long hours. Thousands of subpar factories were built by suppliers, frequently without permissions or even basic safety features like fire exits or grounded wiring, but always with excellent security to keep the workers inside and the looting at bay.

The headquarters of the contractual companies were distant from Bangladesh factories, therefore these workhouses remained hidden and unnoticed. Judy Gearhart, the executive director of the International Labor Rights Forum (ILRF), a nonprofit human rights organisation based in downtown Washington, DC, which was founded in 1986 to advance "the dignity and justice for workers in the global economy," would lead the change. She is a no-nonsense, affable, and unquestionably dedicated to the cause; in 1992, during the NAFTA dispute, Gearhart started defending workers in Mexico. In 2011, she joined the ILRF as executive director. In order to stop child labour, the ILRF has been present in Bangladesh for a long time. However, on April 11, 2005, just after midnight, the badly built nine-story Spectrum Sweater Industries Ltd. plant in the Savar neighbourhood of Dhaka collapsed, leaving sixty-four people dead and eighty injured. Gearhart told me that following it, "our work in the apparel industry really deepened." In order to fight against companies found to have products in any of those factories, we began keeping track of factory fires and collapses and collaborating more closely with the Clean Clothes Campaign and Worker Rights Consortium.

The ILRF has three main strategies: they seek legislative and policy changes, demand greater corporate accountability, and bolster the power and influence of local worker organisations and the working class. However, resistance is still present. The Bangladeshi government receives a substantial amount of cash flow from the clothing industry, not just from income. According to Liana Foxvog, the ILRF's director of organising and communications, in 2018, 10% of Bangladesh parliament members owned garment companies, and 30% had family members who were owners. "So, you can imagine the collusion," Foxvog told me. Moreover, corruption. additionally, the graft. Which, as happened in New York a century ago, results in catastrophe. * The ten-story That's It Sportswear clothing factory caught fire in December 2010, just after Gap representatives had inspected it.

The plant was located outside of Dhaka. It was a common scene: employees defending themselves against shut entrances. Twenty-nine people lost their lives and over one hundred were injured. They were not alone: around 500 Bangladeshi textile workers lost their lives in factory fires between 2006 and 2012. That's It Sportswear manufactured clothing for well-known brands including Gap, Tommy Hilfiger, and Kohl's, therefore the story made international headlines and adjustments were demanded.

The Bangladesh Fire and Building Safety Agreement is a legally enforceable agreement that was hashed up after worker unions and non-governmental organisations met with brands to address workplace safety. It remained unsigned until the winter of 2012, when, more than a year after the incident, ABC News in New York took up the That's It Sportswear story and asked Tommy Hilfiger, the designer, and his top executive about producing such a firetrap. That's when PVH Corp., the company that licences Michael Kors, Sean John, and Speedo and controls the Tommy Hilfiger, Calvin Klein, Van Heusen, IZOD, and Arrow brands, decided to sign the convention. The German retail chain Tchibo joined as well six months later. However, nobody else did, and the deal wouldn't take effect until four businesses were involved.

Twenty-three-year-old Sumi Abedin was at her sewing machine on the fourth floor of the nine-story Tazreen Fashion factory in the Dhaka suburb of Ashulia on a November evening, eight weeks after the safety agreement fell through. She recalled that "a man came up and shouted that there was a fire," but her manager and supervisor reassured everyone that everything was fine. They informed the workers, "There is no fire, just go back and keep working," before locking the door. The fire alarm went off. They were instructed to stay on task by supervisors and security officers, who emphasised that it was just a drill. "I smelled smoke after five or seven minutes," Abedin recalled. She made it to the second story, but that was all she could manage. "I ran to the doors, the stairs, and found that [they were] padlocked... Smoke was coming from downstairs," she added. There were around 1,100 people trapped inside the stairwell because it was "blocked by the fire." There were few, run-down fire escapes, and narrow, open doorways and stairwells. Employees attempted to take down window security bars.

One was successful. He leaped. Then another leaped. Then I leaped, Abedin recalled. Her foot and arm were broken. Her colleague who leaped with her perished instantly. Over 200 people were hurt in total, and at least 117 people lost their lives—nearly half from severe burns. Since the Triangle Shirtwaist Factory fire a century prior, it was the biggest accident to affect the clothing sector. Later, apparel, labels, and documents confirming Disney, Walmart, and Sears had all produced there were discovered by investigators. Tazreen was described by all three as an unapproved source. Surprisingly, according to ILRF's Liana Foxvog, "brands still didn't feel compelled" to sign the Bangladesh Fire and Building Safety Agreement, even after Tazreen, which received a ton of attention in the international media. That gave dubious proprietors of clothing factories, such as Sohel Rana, a sense of positive omnipotence. * SOHEL RANA WAS A THUG. Known as much for his swagger as for his intimidating business techniques, the Bangladeshi operator was in his mid-thirties.

Riding his motorcycle, he would tour Savar with his group of biker friends. Being a political operator, he had the police and public authorities in his pocket, which gave him the freedom to trade drugs and intimidate his adversaries. He earned his money alongside his father, who in the late 1990s sold the family's farmland and purchased a tiny plot in Savar. Rana had taken ownership of part of the land from a former business partner with the help of his armed guards; he had forged the deed to take over another adjacent parcel. The police said nothing. One of Rana's victims stated, "The police were scared." The Rana family built a six-story compound in 2006 to house a bank, shops, and garment factories. The building was built quickly and inexpensively, disregarding safety regulations and zoning restrictions. The residents believe Rana obtained the permission to erect two more stories in 2011 through covert bribery, a prevalent practice in Savar. One former local official acknowledged that the community "grew quickly, and in an unplanned manner." "There are so many buildings like Rana Plaza."

On April 23, 2013, while the five factories housed in Rana Plaza were going about their business, an explosion rocked the structure and tore a second-floor wall apart like a fault line. Workers were busy stitching. Five years later, Shila Begum, a short, thick young woman employed on the fifth floor of Ether Tex Ltd. as a sewing machine operator, recalled, "The crack was so huge I could put my hand in it." Workers, utterly terrified, spilled into the street. An engineer was summoned by management to assess the damage. He desired to condemn the structure right away. Refusing was Sohel Rana, who was meeting with the media at Rana Plaza. He allegedly stated, "The wall's plaster is broken, nothing more." Everyone was told to go home but was told to come back the following morning. "It is not a problem." Approximately eight in the morning. Mahmudul Hassan Hridoy heard a knock on his front door on Tuesday, the following day. Reminding him that they were anticipated at the factory, it was his neighbour and boss.

Hridoy, a pleasant twenty-seven-year-old, was in excellent shape. Two weeks prior, he had left his low-paying job as a nursery school teacher to take a much more lucrative position as a quality inspector for New Wave Style Ltd., a fashion supplier at Rana Plaza. He had also recently tied the knot with his three-year-long girlfriend that weekend. He was strong at arithmetic, so management promised him he would climb the ranks fast. During a 2018 KFC meal in Savar, he informed me, "That's why I joined Rana Plaza." He followed his boss's instructions and reported for duty, just like Shila Begum and everyone else. As we talked outside in the sweltering midday sun on a sidewalk in Savar, she recounted, "I was really in a panic." She explained that they all showed up out of concern that they wouldn't get paid at the end of the month if they didn't.

At the time, Bangladesh's minimum wage was $38 a month, or one-third of what economists define as a living wage, which is the amount required to pay for necessities like clothing, food, and housing. (It was increased to $95 a month in January 2019, which is still half a living wage.) "I was minding my own business, making blue jeans like you are wearing, for a French brand, when the power went out. A couple of minutes later, the generators started." The building shook as the engines rumbled. After that, she hesitated and turned to face me before saying, "It went down." Her dark eyes had lost their brightness, as though someone had taken the light out of her. "My hair got caught in the sewing machine and the concrete ceiling fell on my hand," the woman claimed. Sixteen hours later, after hundreds of emergency personnel had arrived, she was freed by neighbours who had struggled to disentangle her hair but were unable to release her hand. She claimed, "They arrived with pipes and iron rods and pried me out." "They claimed that my insides were disorganised.

Twenty-seven days later, I woke up from my unconscious state. Hridoy was on the seventh level, checking pants, when all of a sudden there was silence and darkness. He remembered that as the generators kicked on, "it felt like the floor under my feet was moving." Then it vanished. He discovered he was pinned behind a concrete pillar when he opened his eyes amid the debris. When everything became clear, he realised he was standing right next to Faisal, one of his closest friends who operated sewing machines on the second floor. Whispering to me, Hridoy said, "I'm not sure how." "I suppose my floor descended to his." Faisal's cranium fractured. "And his mind was overflowing." Hridoy started to cry. He sobbed,

"I can never forget how his head exploded in front of me." "Those memories still haunt me." Rana Plaza was the deadliest factory tragedy in modern history, with 1,134 people killed and 2,500 injured. Begum declared, "I lost all of my friends." "Many were never found." * Helena Helmersson, head of sustainability at H&M, was awakened at five in the morning Stockholm time by her phone ringing. Her Savar point person answered the phone, telling her about the horrific Rana Plaza disaster and reassuring her that H&M did not actually manufacture any of their clothing in Savar.

It was cautioned to her that H&M's contractors might have subcontracted to a Rana Plaza workshop, but this could not be determined until the investigation was finished. Even if H&M was in the clear, consumers and labour rights organisations might still attack the brand as a representation of everything that was wrong with offshoring—the complex and untraceable supply chains, the lack of oversight and safety enforcement, and human rights violations—because it was Bangladesh's biggest apparel exporter. It was seven a.m., two hours later. Helmersson promptly convened with H&M CEO Karl-Johan Persson to meticulously formulate the organisation's reaction. It said, "None of the textile factories in the building produced for H&M." It's critical to keep in mind that Bangladesh's infrastructure is the cause of this calamity, not only the textile sector.

Most companies, on the other hand, said nothing. "The fact that this wasn't any of our suppliers' factories doesn't mean that we are not engaging in the process of contributing to constructive solutions." Foxvog informed me that "no one came forward after Rana Plaza to acknowledge they were manufacturing there." Teams of researchers sifted through the rubble for labels and searched import databases and factory websites for sourcing information for months before determining which brands actually produced there. She called it "a real triangulation." When presented with the facts, Carrefour of France denied producing at Rana Plaza, JCPenney and Lee Cooper/Iconix remained silent, while Walmart asserted that its orders had been subcontracted to Rana Plaza without company authority. When it became evident that clothing from over a dozen US and European brands had actually been manufactured there, the majority of them evaded demands from the relatives and survivors for compensation, and since there were no worker rights agreements in place, there was no legal need to make such payments.

This time, brands were perspiring following a barrage of extremely embarrassing media attention. Tazreen and Rana Plaza's combined might was too much. They needed to take action. Then they recalled the Bangladesh Fire and Building Safety Agreement, an initiative they had blatantly disregarded for the previous two years. In under six weeks, forty-three businesses signed the charter, which was renamed the Accord on Fire and Building Safety. Among them were American Eagle and Fast Retailing, the parent company of Uniqlo. Other signatories included Primark, Inditex, Abercrombie & Fitch, Benetton, and H&M. Numerous other brands, primarily American, objected, citing liability issues. A similar partnership, the Alliance for Bangladesh Worker Safety, was unveiled by Walmart in July. Gap, Target, Hudson's Bay Company (owner of Saks Fifth Avenue and Lord & Taylor), and VF Corporation (owner of Lee Jeans, Wrangler, The North Face, and Timberland) are among the companies that have signed the declaration. However, NGOs believed the Alliance to be less effective and sincere than the Accord, and it was not legally enforceable. According to Foxvog, it was "smaller, and worked with smaller factories."

Additionally, it was a voluntary system that had been shown to be ineffective by decades' worth of fires and collapses. The news reports on Rana Plaza were unvarnished and unavoidable. The ensuing awareness initiatives were quite vociferous. However, Americans' shopping habits for clothing remained unchanged. They spent $340 billion on clothes in 2013—more than twice as much as they did on new vehicles. A significant portion of it was made in Bangladesh, partly by employees of Rana Plaza in the days before the building collapsed. * I visited Bangladesh in April 2018 to check if things had improved in the textile industry following Rana Plaza. In my opinion, the answer is yes. Furthermore, no. To start: sure. Ninety-seven factories have fixed 97,000 safety violations in five years, including missing fire exits, locked doors, and hazardous wiring. Nine hundred have been closed by the authorities for not complying with regulations.

A week prior to my visit, the Stern Center for Business and Human Rights at NYU released a study stating that $1.2 billion in repairs were still required to "remediate remaining dangerous conditions" in Bangladeshi garment factories. The study also called for the creation of a task force to supervise the identification and correction of those violations. Still, there were encouraging signs—the Accord had just been extended for a further three years. I was able to witness the enhancements personally at Rizvi Fashions Ltd., an Accord-compliant factory. The mauve-stuccoed, six-story structure was built in 2014 by former Dhaka stock exchange president Shakil Rizvi on the way to Savar. The 1,450 machines inside were operated by around 2,000 people, who produced between 2 and 2.5 million clothes per month. Rizvi Fashions was quite tidy and safe. Teams of men and women, the majority under thirty, were producing white cotton undershirts for Fruit of the Loom, bubblegum-pink terry shorts with ruffle hems for Deltex Organic, and slate-grey cotton briefs for Primark. To prevent fibre inhalation, everyone—from quality inspectors to sewing machinists—wore a face mask. To keep everything spotless, veiled women constantly pushed broad, mop-like sweepers—homemade Swiffers—up and down the aisles.

The daylight streamed in through wall-length windows, and the fluorescent lights glowed brightly. Even though the temperature outside was already close to 100 degrees, the manufacturing floor had a comfortable temperature thanks to large ventilation fans that cooled and moved the air. The factory was constructed in accordance with Bangladeshi standards at the time, which meant there was no fire safety and exposed wiring hanging from the ceilings. Things took a turn for the worse when Accord inspectors arrived. The wiring is now covered and insulated. There are emergency floodlights, fire extinguishers, axes, and helmet racks; sophisticated fire alarms; monthly fire drills; and fire safety teams, whose leaders are immediately identifiable to employees thanks to Day-Glo yellow vests. The local fire department provides training to one-fifth of the workers so they may learn the fundamentals of first aid, firefighting, and rescue.

As we walked across the plant floor, Anwar Hossain, the manager for compliance, informed me that the process was underway. Sweatshops did not provide other benefits like a daycare facility, an infirmary, or a company-subsidised canteen where employees could purchase drinks and sandwiches for a nominal fee. I peeked in and saw two separate workers' daughters playing together: a seven-year-old and a toddler. Every Friday is a Muslim holy day, and the factory is closed at night. After that, Hossain led me across the parking lot to the "pump room," a separate structure with a high-tech hydraulic system linked to a personal subterranean reservoir holding 150,000 gallons.

He was extremely proud of its installation, as was his staff. Precautions required by the Accord paid off, as Rizvi has never experienced a fire. * THIS DID NOT, HOWEVER, IMPLIED THAT SWeatshops had disappeared from Bangladesh. My guide said to me as we pulled up to one in Dhaka, "I've seen much worse."

The factory we were going to see was situated on a deserted backstreet and was constructed in the early 2000s, but it seemed twice as old because of how run-down it was. "We just drove past several that are much worse." Four older men in uniform who didn't seem very scary were seated at a tiny table at the entryway. A man raised his palm to his face and gave me a little nod, saying as-salamu alaykum, which translates to "Peace be unto you." We ascended the building's lone staircase to reach the reception area on the first floor. It was impossible to imagine the filth daubed on the walls. The boss and his staff welcomed us to tea.

An ancient farm chair with flaking paint was handed to me. On a small stool, my translator sat down. The boss took a seat on a well-worn pink Naugahyde swivel chair behind his Formica-topped desk, stuffed his face till it spilled out the split side seams. The office suite appeared to have been discovered in its entirety on the street. A thin, wide-eyed girl with a magenta sari and tangerine cotton veil passed past without a word. "She's young," I said to my interpreter in a low voice. Quietly, "Fifteen maybe," was his reply. Following a five-minute conversation between our facilitator and the manager, we were taken on a tour. The sole escape route, the stairs, was blocked by large crates of goods destined for Russia.

Large placards with the heading "BUSINESS SOCIAL COMPLIANCE INITIATIVE" on the landing's wall outlined all the labour and safety regulations that the plant was expected to observe in both Bangla and English. The large black plastic cisterns were cracked and half empty, and the red fire buckets filled with debris were next to the doorway. The facilitator murmured, "Those are fake." We went inside the sewing room, which was a long, dim room with shoddy lighting. Over a hundred labourers, ranging in age from the elderly to extremely young—some clearly in their early teens—sat behind dilapidated machines, stitching clothing furiously.

The women had headscarves and saris in bright colours, just like the girl I had seen earlier.

Everybody was barefoot. Despite the placards that read SAFETY FIRST and WEAR A MASK being nailed to the walls, nobody was wearing surgical face masks. The wiring was visible. There were barred windows, many with broken panes. The floors were covered in piles of finished clothing, errant threads, and leftover fabric. It was over 100 degrees Fahrenheit, and it was oppressively hot. Dust was dispersed by tiny fans, although they did not provide much cooling. There were other additional loft-style levels, each with a distinct purpose. Black jeans heaped high on tables in the finishing room.

Shoeless, standing on cardboard pieces, young men and women examined the pants, snipping off threads and patching up holes. Workers in the cutting room used hand tools to draw and cut paper templates instead of the computerised technologies that are now common in aboveboard enterprises. Bolts of cloth strewn randomly throughout the floor, adding further barriers to impede escape in the event that the building catches fire. The fabric cutter was a thin, almost malnourished young man of about twenty. He used an old electric hand-jigsaw, pulling it quickly with his right hand through wads of denim that were five inches thick toward his left, which was only wearing a metal mesh glove, as if that would stop the machine from severing his fingers. Automated textile cutting is seen in modern plants. Our guide informed us that the factory owners were a married couple who worked as ophthalmologists and that they were never there when we were back on the street.

Although he claimed to have produced goods for Walmart and Lidl, he was unsure if they were contracted or subcontracted work. We thanked him for his assistance, climbed back into our worn-out Toyota Uber without seat belts, and headed back into the jam. With the constant beeping and honking of auto rickshaws, scooters, and buses, my translator looked up information about the factory on his phone while we waited. A web page appeared, with pictures of happy employees in a well-lit, tidy workspace and the management group occupying tidy, brand-new office cubicles on the home page. The introduction states that the company was established nine years prior and employed 700 people in addition to 600 equipment. It claimed to have created clothing "100% for export" for companies like CJ Apparel of Great Britain, Roadrunner of Canada, and Camaïeu of France.

I pondered whether any of its clients had ever entered that plant, such as the Russians whose address was on the crates in the stairwell. * Delwar Hossain, the owner of TazrEEN, was ultimately taken into custody and accused of culpable homicide, indicating that he was aware that his carelessness over the factory's security could result in fatalities. The prosecution failed to call witnesses, therefore the trial, which began in 2015, dragged on and was still ongoing by November 2018, the sixth anniversary. In 2016, Sohel Rana and seventeen other people—his parents, the engineer of Rana Plaza, the mayor of Savar, three government inspectors, and the town planner—were accused of a number of offences, including murder. A year later, Rana received a three-year prison sentence for failing to disclose to the Anti-Corruption Commission the full extent of his personal wealth. Appeals to a higher court kept the murder trial and other charges on hold.

Both occurrences were firsts for the Bangladeshi garment sector, notwithstanding their lack of efficiency. According to Gearhart, in 1998, collective bargaining and freedom of association were included in only 15% of firm codes of conduct. It's a given now. It was unimaginable even five years ago for brands to publish supplier lists, and they now compensate for worker deaths. Similar to all previous advancements in Bangladeshi clothing production, Rana Plaza served as the catalyst. Following the tragedy, companies felt suddenly obliged to make reparations for the loss of life or limb, either out of genuine guilt or, more likely, a fear of harm to their reputation. That's not what's referred to as "compensation," Foxvog clarified. The $30 million endowment, hammered out by Clean Clothes Campaign (CCC), was financed by businesses to help lessen the burden for those who suffered catastrophic wounds and the relatives of the deceased. It's known as the "Rana Plaza Arrangement." However, getting those cash has proven to be difficult.

Due to the severity of her injuries, Shila Begum is required to wear a brace on her right forearm and a medical corset. She informed me, "I can barely use my right hand. My kidneys were crushed and damaged." She said she received no help from the government and "nothing from the brands." She is unable to work due to her impairments, and because she is widowed, she has no alternative source of income. Despite the fact that education is technically free, she was forced to withdraw her fourteen-year-old daughter out of school because she could no longer afford books and lunch. She started to cry as she admitted, "I have to beg my family for money." for everyday costs. "I don't want to live anymore when I come here," she remarked, glancing at the empty Rana Plaza lot in front of us. Hridoy, the recent bride, uses a crutch to walk and gets excruciating headaches.

He occasionally rips his hair out when he's sleeping. His wife left him and had an abortion during his protracted recuperation. With tears in his eyes, he continued, "Rana Plaza ruined my life." Still, he has made every effort to reconstruct it. Out of the dozen or so survivors I met in Savar, Hridoy was the only one who had succeeded in obtaining funds from the Rana Plaza Arrangement trust fund.

He opened a tiny drugstore with it. In addition, he established the Savar Rana Plaza Survivors Association, a non-official support organisation with 300 members that gets together in his shop once a month to offer mutual assistance. Such solidarity isn't always sufficient: two association members hanged themselves in their living rooms in 2015 and 2016. The administration continues to oppose unionisation and freedom of association. Factory abuse, both physical and sexual, is still pervasive. Even now, severance pay is not given to workers when manufacturers fail.

Additionally, even in cases where the work is contracted, they remain vulnerable to the brands. Since the summer night of 2016, when Islamic terrorist gunmen attacked a fashionable Dhaka café frequented by foreigners and expats, taking forty hostages and killing twenty, terror has been a persistent concern in Bangladesh. When law enforcement staged a rescue, five militants, two police officers, and two café staff were slain. Fashion representatives alarmed both employees and factory owners by promptly cancelling planned vacations and removing staff from the nation. What would happen to us in the event that buyers decide not to travel to Bangladesh? One mother of two seamstresses wept. Chain hotels in the West strengthened their complexes with x-ray machines, metal detectors, cement barriers, and guards carrying bomb-detecting wands.

The sector recovered. Furthermore, there is the never-ending struggle to give employees a livable salary. They organised rallies and called for instant pay increases in 2016. Owners and the government used force in retaliation, closing fifty-five factories for a week, firing fifteen hundred workers, throwing thirty-five in jail, and detaining twenty-four of them without bond. That was a bad time for us, according to Gearhart. Mark Anner, director of Penn State's Center for Global Workers' Rights, told me that "the industry is obsessed with quarterly returns." "How do you develop a long-term vision if shareholders demand more profits or threaten to pull out every three months?

Never have we had that many workers arrested, held that long, or denied bail." How are workers affected by this trickle-down?or Bangladesh in its entirety? According to Gearhart, "the economy would grow if the workers made a decent wage because they could afford to buy lunch and get a haircut." "Where is today's investment in labourers? Are they only parts of the machine?Fox Sally. Copyright 2012 Paige Green.

Soiled Laundry

Likely, you are reading this while sporting jeans. If not, it's likely that you wore them yesterday. maybe you'll do so tomorrow. Anthropologists estimate that half of the world's population is wearing jeans at any given time. Every year, five billion pairs are made. The typical American purchases four new pairs annually and possesses seven pairs total—one for each day of the week. The French designer Yves Saint Laurent said, "I wish I had invented blue jeans." With the exception of necessities like socks and underwear, blue jeans are the most worn item of clothing ever. "They have expression, modesty, sex appeal, simplicity—all I hope for in my clothes." When the building collapsed, many of the Rana Plaza employees were stitching or checking these. Up until Levi's offshored their jobs, they were the backbone of American textile and apparel manufacture. Every single one of them. Both during their creation and in their afterlife, they are extremely polluting.

All things good, terrible, and wayward in fashion are embodied in jeans. * One of the earliest crops grown by humans, cotton is used to make TRUE BLUE JEANS. It is estimated that domestication began about 3500 BC, while some archaeologists think this may have happened as early as the sixth millennium BC. Cotton was referred to as "a wool exceeding in beauty and goodness that of sheep" by the ancient Greek historian Herodotus. Alexander the Great, the Macedonian king, used cotton, also known as "vegetable wool," for saddle pads and bedding when his army invaded India in 327–326 BC. In the year 63 BC, the official P. Two decades after Lentulus Spinther had sun-blocking cotton awnings built on the theatre for the Apollinarian games, Caesar had cotton tarps erected over the Forum and the route connecting the city's capitol and palace.

Over one hundred countries grow over eighty-two million acres (33.4 million hectares) of cotton annually, producing about sixty billion pounds (121.4 million bales) of the crop. India is the leading producer, followed by China. Cotton is used to make fishnets, coffee filters, book bindings, bandages, disposable diapers, x-rays, and even banknotes, which are made of 25% linen and 75% cotton. But clothes is where cotton is most commonly used: 60% of clothing for women and 75% of clothing for men is made of cotton. In terms of blue jeans, it is 100%. Cotton is one of the most mistreated plants in our garden, despite the comfort and protection it has provided. It's been chopped, sprayed, and overdone to the point where, akin to a Playboy centrefold, it little resembles the original. One of the dirtiest crops in agriculture is nonorganic cotton, sometimes referred to as "conventional" cotton in the industry. Even while conventional cotton is only farmed on 2.5 percent of the world's arable land, one-fifth of insecticides—and more than 10 percent of all pesticides—are used to protect it. Conventional cotton is also very thirsty; to grow one kilogram requires, on average, 2,600 gallons (or 10,000 litres) of water.

The World Health Organization has classified eight out of ten of America's most common cotton insecticides as "hazardous." More water is swallowed during processing—roughly 5,000 gallons for a single T-shirt and pair of pants. By 2030, the world's water supply won't meet demand if fashion manufacturing keeps up its present rate by 40%. The history of denim and jeans is rich in legend. The resilient cotton twill, dyed in indigo, is said to have originated in the southern French town of Nîmes, or de Nîmes as the French refer to it. There are many who claim that Genovese sailors wore blue cotton pants, and that Christopher Columbus of Genoa, also known as "Gênes," utilised the fabric for his sails. Fashion scholars now believe that the modern denim was created in the nineteenth century by textile mills in Manchester, New Hampshire, and was given the name "jean." The fabric's construction has always been straightforward: the warp, or outer side, is made up of two or three yarns, usually dark blue, woven together as one; the weft, or underside, is made up of a single white or pale-hued yarn, giving the fabric a 3-D-like appearance.

A superior quality known as "selvedge" is woven using a continuous weft thread on older, thinner shuttle looms that are half the size of typical ones, which are around sixty inches wide. Aficionados of selvedge jeans roll up their sleeves to showcase the seam edges, which are woven to prevent fraying and give the jeans a "self-edge." Selvedge denim is more solid and tighter than other types of denim. The yarn spun in New Hampshire was initially stained with natural indigo cultivated in the American South. One of the earliest natural colours used by humans is indigo, which is made from the leaves of the Indigofera plant. It was first grown in the United States in the middle of the eighteenth century by slaves owned by English-descended Antiguan Eliza Lucas Pinckney.

On the plantations in South Carolina that her family owned, she planted seeds that her father, the lieutenant governor of Antigua, had sent. Similar to cotton, indigo was grown by slaves and quickly rose to prominence as one of the most profitable crops in the Southern colonies. Up until the early 1870s, denim was a specialty fabric. That changed when a tailor from Reno, Nevada, named Jacob Davis wrote to Levi Strauss, an immigrant of Bavarian descent who had a prosperous dry goods business in San Francisco, asking for assistance in mass-producing his most recent design: work pants with metal rivets at strategic stress points. If Strauss would pay the substantial $68 patenting cost, Davis suggested that the two men might become business partners and manufacture the riveted trousers in San Francisco. Davis said that the pants were so popular among miners, farmers, and labourers that "I cannot make them fast enough." Two variations of the pants—one made of denim and the other of an ecru-coloured canvas known as "duck"—were enclosed by Davis with his letter.

After seeing something he liked, Strauss filed for the patent. 20 May 1873 saw its grant. After relocating to San Francisco, Davis took charge of the first batch of Levi Strauss & Co. jeans in a matter of weeks. The pair's new factory on Market Street employed fifty seamstresses to sew the pants, which were made of denim from Amoskeag Manufacturing Company, a mill in New Hampshire. Most jeans are now designed and sold by Levi Strauss & Co. It is among the most prosperous clothing companies in history. The Vault, the company's archives in Levi's Plaza, its headquarters, an early 1980s brown brick and black glass office structure across from the Embarcadero in San Francisco, is home to the oldest surviving Levis in the world. Tracey Panek, the business historian, is a nice, perceptive middle-aged woman who reminds her of an elementary school librarian. She is in charge of the Vault. Panek took me inside the Vault to see the finest of Levi's vintage collection on a bright fall Friday in 2017. He was wearing black Levi's jeans, a well-worn blue denim jacket, and a bright red turtleneck, which may have been an homage to the brand's iconic scarlet tab.

First up, we have a pair dated 1879. Pulling on her white cotton gloves, Panek carefully took out the pants from one of the three fireproof safes by pulling out a drawer and setting them on a large archive table. Their thighs had a century-old filth ingrained in them that would never, ever come out of the washing. They were broad, short, and coloured a faded chalky blue.

According to Panek, miners would swap and mend their jeans until they were completely devoid of life because they were not inexpensive. She referred to them as the "first sustainable garment," saying that you could fix them and give them to someone else. The "501," so named because of the lot number, was a new jean silhouette that Strauss and Davis unveiled in 1890. Panek showed me some of those old ones. Crafted from an extra-strength denim known as "XX," these pants included buttons for suspenders rather than belt loops, a button fly, and four pockets: three on the front, one on the back, and a small pocket watch insert; the fifth pocket was added on the derriere in 1901.

The 501's silhouette hasn't changed since then. Strauss became one of the wealthiest people in California thanks to the proceeds from his blue jeans business. He looked well in it, too. He was about five foot six and slightly round, and he always looked sharp in a black broadcloth suit with a top hat, silk tie, and waistcoat. He didn't wear the jeans that his business made. When he passed away in 1902 at the age of 73, he bequeathed a large portion of his almost $1.667 million inheritance to regional charities and his four nephews took over the company. He also never got married, saying, "My entire life is my business." Sigmund Stern, one of them, and Walter Haas, Stern's son-in-law, assumed leadership roles. The button fly and suspender buttons were swapped out with zippers and belt loops, modernising the denim design. Additionally, they added a new supplier in the South, the Cone brothers' White Oak Cotton Mills in Greensboro, North Carolina, even though they were still purchasing their denim from Amoskeag Mills. Like Strauss, Moses and Ceasar [sic] Cone were brothers from Bavaria who created Cone Mills in the mid-1890s.

After learning of Strauss's success in the West, they recognized a lucrative economic potential and converted an abandoned steel mill—named Proximity Manufacturing because it was located near gins and cotton fields—into a denim factory. They opened a second operation, White Oak Cotton Mills, in 1905, taking their name from a magnificent two-hundred-year-old oak that stood close by. The German chemist Adolf von Baeyer created synthetic indigo, which BASF (Badische Anilin und Soda Fabrik) began selling in 1897 and used to dye a large portion of the denim made there. Synthetic indigo was not susceptible to weather damage or blight, unlike natural indigo. Indeed, it was composed of a variety of chemicals, some of which we now know to be environmentally hazardous. Still, it was more affordable and reliable. This made it possible for mills such as Cone to weave and dye denim for a whole year. The natural indigo industry had collapsed by 1914 and would never fully rebound. Moses was referred to as the Denim King, and White Oak eventually grew to be the world's biggest denim manufacturer.

The Cones and the nephews of Levi Strauss met in 1915 to talk about obtaining denim from White Oak. The two sides reached a quick deal, which was marked with what is known as "the Golden Handshake" in history. After that, Cone provided Levi Strauss with fabric solely for their 501 pants. And the appeal of blue jeans increased gradually until it unexpectedly took off in the 1970s, thanks to Seventh Avenue of all places. Designer jeans are a new fashion category created by New York's fashion designers in response to the women's liberation movement and the growing popularity of more casual attire. Designer jeans epitomised the hedonism and Madison Avenue swagger of the era with their slim-cut legs and seats that cupped the rear. According to Calvin Klein, "Jeans are sex." "The tighter they are, the better they sell." To emphasise this point, Brooke Shields, an actress and model, was fifteen years old when Klein cast her in his 1980 jeans campaign.

Do you wish to know what stands in my way of wearing my Calvins? Wearing his pants and a taupe blouse, she sat spread-eagled and purred in her innocent voice. "Nothing." The advertisement was so offensive that ABC and CBS's New York stations quickly rejected it. However, Klein had already accomplished its goal: in the week that followed the advertisement's release, he sold 400,000 pairs, and a month later, he sold 200,000 pairs. Sales of jeans soared to unprecedented levels: in 1981 alone, over half a billion pairs were bought. * A significant portion of jeans sold up to the 1970s were composed of stiff, shrink-to-fit, or "," denim. (Preshrunk cotton, also referred to as "sanforized," has been around since the early 1930s; however, the denim industry did not adopt it until the 1960s, when prewashing became standard practice.) To fit jeans, one would either buy them a size or two larger, wash them, or, better yet, put them on and soak in a bathtub full of water. Truly.

All you had to do was wear them to make them softer. A great deal. It took well over a year for the jeans to break in correctly. The hems and pocket edges might begin to fray after a few years—years—or a knee might split apart. With some whiskering—the sunburst-like streaks that emanate from the fly—the fabric faded to a powdered blue. You have to put in a lot of time and effort to make your jeans seem just amazing. That is, until stonewashing became widely accepted in the 1980s. When the denim was sufficiently worn down, unwashed jeans were placed into industrial washers equipped with pumice stones and tumbled. (The Los Angeles-based casualwear brand Guess was known for its seven-hour stone washing process, which is now regarded as an environmental horror.) Jeans were occasionally further distressed using acid, sandpaper, rasps, and files to replicate the previously hard-won wear and tear.

The entire procedure was called "finishing," and it was carried out in large buildings known as "washhouses," which currently handle hundreds of pairs of jeans every day. Certain washhouses are very sophisticated and adhere to stringent worker safety and environmental standards. This is particularly the case in Los Angeles, the epicentre of the American jeans industry. However, many do not, as I witnessed on a humid April morning in Ho Chi Minh City in 2018. Vietnam's textile and clothing industries are both ancient and modern. Although local women have long spun and woven silk into beautiful fabrics for clothing and the house, the country did not have many factories like Arkwright's that produced fabric and clothes by the ton until the middle of the 20th century. For many years, Vietnam's GDP was primarily based on the apparel and textile industries. Although I saw a few factories during my visit in early 1993, the country's economy was primarily based on agriculture, as evidenced by the emerald lawn of rice paddies that covered much of the country. Globalisation and trade agreements altered that terrain.

Approximately 6,000 textile and apparel manufacturing businesses employed 2.5 million people in Vietnam as of 2018, contributing over $30 billion in revenue and about 16 percent of the nation's exports. Experts predict that by 2020, that last amount will increase to $50 billion. Jeans finishing takes up a lot of the work. Vietnam's jeans manufacturing revenue was $600 million in 2012; by 2021, it is predicted to treble. Together with a denim expert from the area, I pulled up to a dilapidated warehouse-style plant hidden behind an impregnable fence on the industrial outskirts of Ho Chi Minh City. It was an easy hundred degrees outside and there were roughly two hundred young Vietnamese labourers working under subpar fluorescent lighting inside.

Huge fans hummed in an attempt to chill the space. It failed to work. Dollies and metal tables were covered with mounds of flawless midnight-blue pants. They were taken by young men dressed in butter-yellow T-shirts, jeans-like pants, and knee-high rubber boots, who then jammed them into two dozen enormous washing machines. Out of the machines, wads of sopping jeans were removed by other young males wearing boots. There was one inch of navy blue water on the ground. The men's hands were discoloured black, and they lacked gloves. Older models of some of the machines needed twenty litres, or five gallons, of water to wash one kilogram, or three pairs, of jeans. Others, using somewhat more than a gallon of water—five litres—per kilogram of jeans, were less chubby. According to my guide, manufacturers are aware of how wasteful this is. And expensive: effluent needs to be treated; fortunately, Vietnamese washhouses can no longer dump directly into the waterways. On the opposite side of town, I noticed a canal into which years' worth of jean-washhouse garbage had been dumped.

Now the water looked like tar, and I felt like throwing up due to its stench. However, persuading factory owners to alter their practices is difficult. According to a jeans specialist, "their business is about washing, not about worrying about the environment." After being loaded into huge crates and transported to a different area, the drenched jeans were placed inside large dryers. To simulate whiskering, some of the jeans underwent chemical treatment and were then cooked in a massive oven. This is known as the "dry process." In the distressing room, young men and women were sanding jean knees and thighs by hand, much the way a carpenter works on wood, while wearing sky-blue T-shirts (each department had a specific colour). While some people avoided breathing in denim dust by wearing surgical masks, the majority did not. Each duo went from virgin to ruined in less than a minute, demonstrating the startling enthusiasm with which they approached their mission. The workers were so focused that they were oblivious to everything around them and did not even communicate. Their income would be withheld if they made a mistake. Without overtime, sanders processed at least 400 pairs of jeans every day, six days a week, when I visited. That was the distressers for hands. Even faster were the machine distressers in action.

One woman I saw was using what appeared to be an enormous dental drill to attack cutoff shorts, and she let out a scream so high-pitched it could break crystal. In ten seconds, she ground those shorts' hems and front and rear pockets to a stylishly holey state. Every minute, six pairs. during the entire day. It was difficult not to sneeze in the room where she was uncovered. All of this reportedly paled in comparison to the washhouses of Xintang, a town in Guangdong Province, China, which bills itself as the "jeans capital of the world." Of the 300 million pairs of jeans produced annually by 200,000 garment workers in Xintang's 3,000 factories and workshops, 800,000 pairs are produced every day. The East River, a tributary of the Pearl River, is where companies dumped their dye waste after the local water treatment plant collapsed many years ago. It became opaque, making it uninhabitable for aquatic life. Lead, copper, and cadmium concentrations in the riverbed are high, according to Greenpeace's research.

The streets of Xintang have blue dust. In addition, a number of garment workers have reportedly experienced lung infections, infertility, and skin rashes. * Cotton specialist Sally Fox told me that this didn't HAVE to be the case. On an early autumn morning, we were seated at a basic wooden table in Fox's double-wide trailer on her 130-acre property, Viriditas Farm, in the Capay Valley, northwest of Sacramento. Stacks of cardboard containers and rows of oak filing cabinets filled with cotton dossiers, including studies, orders, and samples, flanked the living room. There were open windows. Her merino sheep bleated in the pasture, a rooster croaked in the barnyard, and the north wind rippled through the shade tree in front, breaking the silence. Fox, who stood five feet seven, had an honest smile on her face and a rime-white bob. She was wearing caramel denim pants and a water-blue chambray tunic.

Her face was clean, without makeup and perfectly lined for her sixty-one years; her lovely turquoise eyes shone. I had gone to see Fox because, in the business, she is regarded as the originator of contemporary organic cotton. She was raised in Northern California and began spinning wool, cotton, and other materials when she was twelve years old, using the money she earned from babysitting. She worked on the development of natural pest control strategies in the Gambia during her 1979–1980 Peace Corps assignment. She has been breeding and growing coloured organic cotton in Arizona and California for the past forty years or so. Since Gossypium was first cultivated, coloured cotton has been a thing. It comes in a variety of colours, including brown, tan, green, and blue. During our conversation in her trailer, Fox informed me that the Chinese cultivated nankeen, a pale-yellow variant favoured in the American colonies and used for textiles.

After completing her master's degree, she started working with independent plant breeder Robert Dennett in the Davis, California, area. "Everyone wanted nankeen gold trousers." One day, she was cleaning the greenhouse when she opened a drawer and discovered a brown cotton bag. She remembered the fibre to be short, weak, and scratchy. However, it enchanted her, and she reasoned that since it wouldn't require dying, others would desire it if it could be spun. In Dennett's greenhouse, she planted potted seeds that she had ordered from the USDA. Fox planted a quarter of an acre of ground close to Bakersfield, the epicentre of California cotton growing, since she was so happy with the way they turned out. She found that the tannins that gave the cotton its colour also made it naturally resistant to disease and insects, so she farmed organically back when "no one was doing organic cotton." "The next year," she recalled, "I rented an acre, then five, then eleven, and on and on." "No one."

To market her coloured cotton, which she called FoxFibre, she founded Natural Cotton Colours Inc. She also started working with independent fashion designers and securing production deals. One concerned Levi's. Fox's cotton helped create a caramel-coloured denim that her buddy Dan DiSanto, a designer for Levi's at the time, used for a new line. That denim was what Fox was wearing the morning we met at her property. Fox and Levi's worked out a three-year agreement. She would provide farmers in West Texas colourful cotton seeds, and the farmers would grow the cotton, spin it, and weave it into denim at a mill they jointly controlled as a cooperative. After that, Levi's would purchase the finished denim and make apparel out of it. Levi's purchased the denim from the farmers who had planted 100 acres of Fox's seed the previous year. In the second, a thousand acres was added to the order. And it was three thousand acres in the third year.

Fox said, "The farmers made so much money." Like Levi, "they were really happy." She said that the jackets and jeans were "wildly popular." Bob Haas, the head of Levi's and Strauss's great-great-grandnephew, told Fox that "this could change the world" when she surpassed the 1,000-acre threshold. "It will take me two years, but I could do it," she replied. "Please do it," he added. "If you could get a hundred thousand acres' worth of seed, I can do it, I can make it happen." Fox and Haas did not draft a contract this time. She told me, "I bet my business on it. I just made it my goal because I wanted to be part of the reduction of this enormous environmental disaster." While Fox was working on the project, Levi's experienced a management crisis. "I got all the seed, and I paid a million dollars to do it and prepared to plant the seeds for one hundred thousand acres," Fox said. Has launched a leveraged takeover in 1996, when the brand was reporting sales of a record-breaking $7.1 billion annually—more than Nike.

A number of relatives received voting rights as part of the acquisition, but the company also took on $3.3 billion in debt that was listed on the stock market, placing it in a risky financial position. It turns out that 1996 marked the peak of Levi's revenue; in the years that followed, sales abruptly declined as the company lost market share to start-ups facing intense competition. People rolled their heads. When Fox travelled to San Francisco to meet with the new executive team—Haas was still the CEO—she said that "the vice president went on this rant about how he hated brown and green." Have you ever come across a green car?"Levi's cancelled the cotton order," he declared. Natural Cotton Colours, Fox's business, filed for Chapter 11 bankruptcy.

She silently stared across the Northern California plains from her double-wide's window. "I lost everything." * For a large portion of the 20th century, the clothing industry regarded Levi's as a brand with moral integrity. This was due in part to the fact that the corporation was based in politically liberal San Francisco and that its owners, the Haases, were devoted Jews who continued their father's legacy of giving.

Walter Haas Jr., the CEO of Levi's, hired a religious ethicist in the 1970s to give him advice on how to implement more ethical business practices. The business is well known for having abandoned operations in Indonesia in the middle of the 1970s due to the pervasive corruption there and for declining to enter the South African market due to the racial apartheid laws of the government. One of the earliest American companies to address the AIDS crisis was Levi's, which developed policies to support staff members who were HIV positive in the early 1980s. Bob, the son of Walter Jr. and a former Ivory Coast Peace Corps volunteer, continued this philosophy when he took over as president in 1984.

In 1990, he stated, "It is really more than paternalism." But now the company is failing. "A company's values—what it stands for, what its people believe in—are crucial to its competitive success." The fashion consumer had moved on to hot new specialised labels, while the teen market had shifted to hipper names like Gap and Tommy Hilfiger. Josie Esquivel, an apparel analyst at Morgan Stanley Dean Witter, claimed at the time that Levi's "lost sight of who they are" as a result of the company starting to sell at discount stores like Kohl's in an attempt to make up for the sharp decline in revenue. Its moral compass had vanished along with its cachet. The company's values vanished along with the sales. Levi's declared in 1997, three years after NAFTA, that it would close fourteen operations in the US and Europe due to excessive labour expenses. I learned about the harsh impact on workers and the communities where Levi's had operated for many years from Annabelle Nichols, a staunchly conservative Southern woman who was 74 years old when I met her in 2016.

Nichols had worked at Levi's Cherry Street plant in Knoxville, Tennessee, for the first forty years of her career as a garment manufacturer. Levi's largest plant in North America was located in Knoxville. It was split into four sections, each roughly the size of a football field, and separated by cement-block walls and steel sliding doors when it first opened in 1953 in a former tobacco warehouse. Ninety-five percent of the workers were women. They started work at 7 a.m. Monday through Friday from 6 a.m. to 3:30 p.m. producing 20,000 pairs of blue jeans every day on Saturdays in addition to khakis "and dress slacks," according to Nichols. Men made up the remaining 5% of the workforce, and they were managers. There were no female managers; instead, women in charge of employees were called "supervisors," and they were subordinate to and paid less than men.

At the age of nineteen, Nichols began working in 1961. Seven years later, she was promoted to supervisor. The day before election day, Monday, November 3, 1997, as the plant floor clattered with its customary Gatling-gun-like racket, an authoritative voice called out over the public address system, requesting that employees switch off their equipment. The voice returned, this time with a more melancholy tone, once the large room had quieted down: "We have some devastating news... the factory will cease operations by the end of the year." Employees started crying at their workstations. At the time, 37,500 workers were employed by Levi's in more than fifty factories across the globe. Of those, thirty-two were located in the United States.

Canada was home to five. Levi's declared that it would close all eleven locations—including Cherry Street—immediately. That was equivalent to about 6,400 production workers, or 34% of Levi's North American workforce, of which 1,800 were located in Knoxville. Levi's insisted that it was not outsourcing the labour, citing consumer expenditure on clothing as the reason for the downsizing, which decreased from 7% of income in the 1980s to 4% in the 1990s. Within a year, Levi's had laid off almost forty-three percent of its global workforce; to compensate its "dislocated workers," the business paid hefty severance packages and job coaching. Nothing really lessened the layoffs' misery. After a brief period of retirement, Nichols went back to work as a production manager for Smithville, Tennessee-based Omega Apparel, a company that makes military uniforms. Not everybody was as fortunate. She informed me, "We lost a lot of good people. Several passed away right after." * Levi's sales continued to plummet; in just three years, revenue dropped by 28% to $5.1 billion. According to John Ermatinger, president of Levi's American business, the company announced additional facility closures in order to "give the company greater flexibility."

The Union of Needletrades, Industrial and Textile Employees' secretary-treasurer, Bruce Raynor, saw through Levi's plan and called it "[Levi's] decision to join the race to the bottom." To lead a successful turnaround and carry out the closures, Levi's appointed fifty-two-year-old Philip Marineau as CEO. Marineau was most recently the president and CEO of Pepsi-Cola North America. He led the business as its first non-Strauss family member. The plan was straightforward: Levi's "had to go from a company that was a self-manufacturer to a creator, marketer and distributor of apparel," said Marineau. (Haas remained chairman.) Marineau said he'd use the same methods that he used to sell Gatorade and Mountain Dew, since, he claimed, without irony, soft drinks "aren't dissimilar to the fashion business." Put differently, it planned to outsource all production, which would then go out to contract again, and so on. This required closing the final Levi's-owned locations, including the "Mother Factory" on Valencia Street in San Francisco, which first opened its doors in 1906, and a plant that had been in operation for 43 years in Blue Ridge, Georgia, an Appalachian Mountain hamlet with 1,400 residents.

A year prior, Levi's had already let go of three hundred employees at Blue Ridge. It was now giving the last four hundred people pink slips. These were manual labour positions. For jobs like sewing zippers into jeans, inserting rivets, and creating belt loops, the majority of workers were paid between $8 and $14 per hour. A few earned as low as $20,000 annually. Levi's compensated for his meagre income, nevertheless, by giving generously to the public library, Little League teams, schools, hospitals, and nursing homes. It donated $10,000 to the fire department in 2001 for a new communications system, and it provided little bags filled with grooming supplies or modest bills to elderly residents of the community health centre every Christmas. Throughout the years, the corporation has paid several thousand dollars for the county's first mobile defibrillator, as well as helping to cover the cost of curling irons for a cosmetology course, a Jaws of Life hydraulic rescue tool, and field lights at the stadium. Doug Davenport, the principal of the secondary school, stated, "They've just allowed us to have a lot of things we couldn't have had." That was done.

Blue Ridge came to represent the social and economic devastation that short-sighted, profit-driven decisions made in boardrooms—such as offshoring—caused in America's local manufacturing towns. To assist former Levi's employees in finding new employment, the state established an employment agency. This was not an easy feat, as few of them held a high school diploma. Because former industrial families could no longer afford the $20 enrollment fee, local children were not taking swimming lessons at the county rec centre. When more people relocated in search of employment, the student body shrank and the school board was forced to fire teachers. Public services had to be decreased as a result of declining revenue. Bernie Hodgkins, the director of recreation for Fannin County, stated that finances will be tight. Marineau continued to move on despite Levi's receiving negative coverage in the national news for leaving Blue Ridge and saying, "It's going to devastate this little county, I feel." In complete contrast.

He let go of 25,000 Levi's workers in total. "From a justice standpoint, there's no reason to say that the person in San Antonio deserves that job versus the person in Pakistan," he said in an interview with the San Francisco Chronicle, defending his actions. Marineau reportedly made $6.3 million in salary, bonuses, and long-term incentive payouts in 2004 while firing all those people, and he was eligible for an additional $4 million bonus over the following two years. He resigned at the age of sixty at the end of those two years. His annual pension was $1.2 million. Levi's sales were also falling, coming in at $4.19 billion, about half of what they had reached a decade earlier. * Sally Fox got back together after her bankruptcy. She exchanged her farm in Kern County for the farm in Brooks, where we were seated that October morning, through an "ag exchange." "Same amount of acreage, but this is much prettier," she remarked, admiring her undulating landscape outside the window. She brought her seeds, a truck, and a travel trailer, which she lived in until 2003 when she moved into a double-wide. To keep the lines going, she continued to breed and cultivate little amounts of cotton. She made all of her money from her internet sales of the yarns, socks, and sweaters that she made. Everything is entirely natural. Cotton was made by Mother Nature to be a perennial.

According to Fox, it "wants to grow and become a huge tree" in its first year, then it blooms the next year. Low-fertile soils will force the plant to flower, therefore you must stress it the first year by not giving it enough water or fertiliser. Because of this, cotton has traditionally been associated with poor soil; it was a crop you planted on your field as a last resort before applying a lot of manure or cover crops. Cotton could be planted to produce income even if you lacked the funds to restore soil quality. However, in the 1980s, BASF created Pix, a chloride-based growth regulator, which effectively made cotton an annual by inducing blooming when sprayed to the plants. This scientific discovery completely changed the cotton industry because, outside of the European Union, where production is mostly concentrated in Greece and the Iberian Peninsula, farmers are paid by the yield rather than the acre. Farmers started heavily watering and irrigating their plants to encourage development before applying Pix. According to Fox, "you could go from one production bale per acre to six bales overnight."

The majority of conventional cotton growers were employing Pix by the 1990s. A commercial variety of genetically modified cotton known as "Roundup Ready Cotton" was introduced by the multinational American agrochemical and biotechnology company Monsanto in 1997 to combat weeds. The cotton seeds were designed to withstand heavy applications of Roundup, a glyphosate-based herbicide that is part of Monsanto's "broad spectrum" product line. Roundup would essentially destroy everything save cotton. Farmers must buy both since they are necessary for each other to function effectively. Rivals of Monsanto have also developed their own versions. Furthermore, conventional farmers have accepted it: 94% of American cotton in 2018 was genetically modified. Up to 99 percent of the cotton farmed was in Alabama, Arkansas, Louisiana, Mississippi, and Missouri; 100 percent was in Georgia. The most widely used herbicide in the world, roundup makes up 40% of the market for glyphosate weed killer worldwide. Environmentalists who supported fashion had doubts about the benefits of all this scientific advancement for the planet. Yvon Chouinard, the founder of Patagonia, studied the effects of Roundup in 1994 and came to the deadly conclusion that it should only be used on organic cotton by 1996.

Twenty years later, Chouinard's worries were realised when the World Health Organization's International Agency for Research on Cancer declared in 2015 that Roundup and other glyphosate-based herbicides were "probably carcinogenic to humans." In 2018, Bayer acquired Monsanto and declared that it would discontinue using the century-old name, which activists had come to associate with corporate evil. Farmers use the carbonate pesticide Bayer's Aldicarb to fight the many pests that plague cotton. Among the most commonly used pesticides is aldicarb. Furthermore, it has been shown to be toxic to both people and animals. In excessive amounts, it can be fatal. Exposure can cause tremors, headaches, nausea, tears, sweating, and blurred vision. Aldicarb has been documented to be used by burglars in South Africa to poison pets. It's concerning to learn that sixteen US states have water tables with residues of aldicarb.

The Environmental Protection Agency developed a plan to phase out Aldicarb in 2018 during the administration of President Obama. But the website detailing the phaseout was out of date in 2017, the year the Trump administration took over the government agency. * Denim's popularity endures despite all the negative connotations it bears in the world of fashion. David Weil, dean of Brandeis University's Heller School for Social Policy and Management, told me that "the pressure of capital markets, private and public," is one of the many factors contributing to this cycle of fashion purchasing. The entire supply chain has been tainted, from labour to raw materials. He declared, "What is considered appropriate behaviour has eroded." In the end, he added, brands will have to accept the idea of reduced earnings. He believes that in order to change it, state and federal agencies must bring "the tops of these companies to the table and get them to have a greater incentive to set pricing structures that behave differently." Additionally, he stated, "consumers will have to pay somewhat more."

In other words, the industry needs to wake up if customers want $11 clothing that they will feel good about. Weil claimed that today's fashion executives "dictate everything they want in their supply chain—a specificity not only of the product but product delivery, barcode, shipping containers—to an incredible degree." When the dyes aren't correct, they closely monitor it and will return an order. However, he went on, "you're not working in a building like Rana Plaza, therefore maybe it's unrealistic to make sure that the fire emergency exits laws are followed. Natalie Chanin harvesting cotton on the Lentz farm in Trinity, Alabama. He stated, "Either you start attacking that piece of this problem, through a combination of consumer and NGO pressure, and cooperation of governments," or you come up with "a different production model, entirely." By Rinne Allen, © 2012.

Form to Field

Florence, a town of 39,000 people, is located in the northeastern corner of Alabama, across the Tennessee River from Muscle Shoals, the epicentre of R&B recording. Florence was known as the World's Cotton T-Shirt Capital before NAFTA. Fashion designer Natalie Chanin told me, over heirloom BLTs and iced tea at her farm-to-table restaurant, The Factory Café, situated in Bldg. 14, one of twenty massive one-story former factories in an industrial park on the outskirts of town, that "they used cotton that was grown around here." English-fair, "eighth or ninth generation" southern, and a Florence native, Chanin has a plane of ash-white hair, cheerful hazel eyes capped by crow-black brows, and a voice like Tupelo honey. She can still clearly recall the days when her city was a thriving hub for the garment industry. Tee Jays Manufacturing Co., the third-largest employer in the Shoals, used to be located where we were having lunch.

Before NAFTA, in the early 1990s, Tee Jays paid out $50 million in payroll annually. "The dye house was back behind us, and there was a knitting machine in this building," Chanin stated. "This was a sewing floor," she said, sweeping her hand over the expansive area where we were seated. Simply endless lines of equipment. Hemmers, hundreds and hundreds of them. Walt Disney, Ralph Lauren, and Tommy Hilfiger were all employed locally. With the ratification of NAFTA, US T-shirt manufacturing relocated abroad. Regional producers such as Tee Jays stopped their business. Terry Wylie, the company's previous owner, told me that NAFTA "ruined the company." Florence fell into a financial and social catastrophe, just like a large portion of the textile-dependent South. Five thousand people worked in this two-block radius in 1993, according to Chanin.

Furthermore, it did not encompass all service sectors, such as eateries, childcare facilities, and petrol stations.

This town used to have twenty dye houses. Twenty-five years later, Chanin and her friend Billy Reid, a fashion designer from Louisiana, are helping Florence live up to its nickname, "Renaissance City." At The Factory, Chanin manages Alabama Chanin, a women's wear company that specialises in elegant tailoring and flowing organic-cotton dresses, both of which are made in the area. When I went there in 2018, there were twelve Reid shops around the country. Reid's headquarters are located on Court Street, the town's major thoroughfare. His trademark style is what one fashion writer for the New York Times called "whiskey-soaked style"; selvedge jeans of superior quality, tattered work shirts, clean linen slacks, and crinkly seersucker blazers are all prevalent.

Chanin and Reid have surrounded themselves with a tribe of young urbanites to staff their businesses; Reid employs seventy people in addition to Chanin's thirty. Numerous trendy new enterprises, including gastropubs, boutique hotels, a microbrewery, and Single Lock Records—co-founded by local Grammy-winning musician John Paul White—have emerged as a result of this inflow of creative types. Reid hosts Shindig, a three-day public celebration of southern cuisine, music, fashion, and culture, every August that draws guests from all across the South. A fun benefit dinner for a few hundred people at The Factory Café, hosted by Chanin to promote the Southern Foodways Alliance, a regional centre for the study of southern food culture, started off Shindig No. 8, which I attended in August 2016. Chanin and Reid are part of a growing global movement known as "slow fashion," which is made up of makers, designers, retailers, and manufacturers who have drastically slowed down their pace and financial goals in response to globalisation and fast fashion.

This has allowed them to concentrate more on producing products with intrinsic value, carefully selecting their clientele, and lessening their environmental impact. Their desire to raise the standard of living for their family and workers is another motivator behind this quiet revolution. Localization and regionalism are favoured above mass-ification by slow fashion. It embraces new technologies to make production more efficient and clean, while also upholding tradition and craftsmanship. She supports like-minded fashion folk as best she can; she has sourced cotton from Sally Fox, collaborated with young Nashville-based designer Elizabeth Pape of the direct-to-consumer Elizabeth Suzann label, and is good friends with and a sounding board for New York-produced women's wear brand Maria Cornejo. Chanin said it's about treating workers well and "buying from the person down the street whose face you know and love."

Chanin often strives to answer questions from budding designers who ask how she manages to make things work. "It's crucial to assist the future generation," she remarked. She also gives public tours of The Factory every day at 2:00 p.m. She also thinks that education is important, saying, "We try to be as transparent as possible." She publishes needlework books and launched an outreach program called the School of Making at The Factory. "Design school students who come to us know nothing more than how to draw, send their drawings, and receive finished clothing back," Chanin remarked. "A lot of critical knowledge that has been lost—a real lack of understanding of how clothes are made" is what Chanin observed when she produced Stitch, a short documentary about the craft of southern quilting, in 2001 to coincide with the launch of her debut collection.

She has been recording an oral history of sewing in the South since 2016 in collaboration with the University of Mississippi's Center for the Study of Southern Culture. Additionally, she shared part of the research at her first Project Threadway's Symposium in April 2019, which is a yearly celebration of "manufacturing, music, and community" with an emphasis on cotton, material culture, textile history, and women in the workforce. It is essential for us to "be able to manufacture our garments," according to Chanin, who sees her educational projects as a means of "preserving" needlecraft—"a skill that is fading away in this country." If we lose the knowledge of handcrafts like sewing, she questions, "What happens to the culture?* CHANIN GREW UP in the area of cotton farms. Her paternal grandfather was a carpenter, her maternal grandfather was employed by the Tennessee Valley Authority, and both grandfathers were farmers. She laughed and continued, "My mother always throws out that she picked cotton to buy her school clothes."

The military issued undergarments were manufactured at the Sweetwater Mill in Florence by Chanin's maternal grandmother and great-grandmother. Her father worked as a commercial contractor and carpenter, and her mother taught maths in middle schools. They all imparted to Chanin the value of being self-sufficient. Her grandmothers taught her how to sew and did the sewing at home; one of them "made everybody's underwear, nightgowns, everything," she recalled. Chanin used to spend a lot of time playing dress-up with old clothes, capes, and shawls in her grandmother's attic. She told me, "That's how I fell in love with clothes." Zach was born when she was twenty years old, and she attended North Carolina State University to study fashion and textile design. After graduating in 1987, she moved to New York to work on Seventh Avenue as a design assistant for a junior sportswear company. She had to reassess her job goals after what she experienced there. "I travelled a lot, and I saw a lot of things that I don't think are right—things that you shouldn't want people to do," the woman remarked. She also heard stories of horror.

Chanin said that one of her friends who worked for Gap "told me she visited a dye house in India and the dye was just pouring into a river." Children were fetching and consuming water fifteen feet downstream from the source. They were consuming blue dye. The river had a blue colour. She relocated to Vienna, Austria, in 1990 and started working as an MTV stylist. "If that's how I have to make fashion, then I don't want to make fashion," she thought to herself. In 2000, she went back to New York for what was meant to be a sabbatical, staying at the Hotel Chelsea. She went to Goodwill every day and bought T-shirts. She would dissect them, reassemble them using collage, and embellish them with unique embroidery with exposed knots and trailing threads. Her inspiration came from an old corset she found at the Twenty-Sixth Street flea market. She recalled, "It had been cut away and added to, and I couldn't figure out what was inside and what was outside." "I flipped the T-shirts inside out, exposing the work on the underside, since that's how I felt about my life at that point—inside out, upside down, and sideways. And that established our style. Chanin needs assistance to create a suitable collection.

She made a call to the Garment District workshops. "I tried to get them to do the elaborate embroidery, but no one could comprehend my words," the woman remarked. Alabama has a long history of quilting, carried on by such associations as the Gee's Bend Collective and, until 2012, the Freedom Quilting Bee. "Then I realised it looked like a quilting stitch, and if I wanted to get it made as I wanted, I needed to come home to Alabama, where people still quilted," she said. She looked to rent a home in the countryside where she grew up because she thought that is where she would find the quilters. Adjacent to Chanin's own residence, Chanin's aunt just acquired a red brick house that his grandfather had constructed in 1949 for his closest friend. After moving there, Chanin organised a workstation and a few sewing machines and hired quilters to perform her embroidery.

Project Alabama got underway. Once there were enough items of clothing ready for photos and sales, Chanin assembled a tiny catalogue, referred to as a "look book" in the industry, and sent it off to stores. Julie Gilhart, the fashion director of Barneys at the time, found one on her desk. Gilbert's specialty was identifying and developing up-and-coming designers. She visited Chanin at the Chelsea after being intrigued by the look book, which Gilhart described to me as "beautiful and artistic." What she saw pleased her. Gilhart remarked, "Natalie's T-shirts had a lot of style to them, and her collection had purpose—she was encouraging crafted culture and employing a lot of women in Alabama." Many other businesses followed, including Ron Herman in Los Angeles and Browns in London. "I loved that, and we ran with it." The T-shirts might cost up to $400 each at retail. Gilhart said that Natalie was supported by the designer client. From then, Chanin created a more comprehensive collection of dresses and suits in the 1930s and 1940s, modelled after Blanche DuBois's appearance in A Streetcar Named Desire. "They sold very well."

All were created by Florence seamstresses using recycled fabrics or organic cotton. Chanin flew back and forth between Florence and New York, bringing the collection to Paris Fashion Week twice a year to show it off to foreign shops in a hotel room on the Left Bank. At the time, she sold wholesale products overseas for eighty percent of her total revenue. Around this time, I had the pleasure of seeing Chanin in one of the West Hollywood villas constructed by Craig Ellwood at the Chateau Marmont. She came to town to generate business during L.A. Fashion Week. A mutual acquaintance invited me over, and I brought my four-year-old daughter with me. With a cotton jersey in her lap, a threaded needle in her right hand, and her left hand moving down the strands as though she were massaging them, Chanin sat on the mid-century modern sofa. She told my daughter, "This is called 'loving the thread,'" a Southern ritual to prepare the thread for stitching. Twisting the strands until they are taut is the process of spinning. "Too much tension causes your thread to tangle when you sew," the woman explained. "Loving your thread" is a practice I learned. When you drag it between your fingers, the oils on your skin coat the strands, releasing stress.

She showed my daughter how to do this, and the two of them sat there, slowly and painstakingly pulling thread through their fingertips. Then it doesn't tangle as much. Sales for Chanin were respectable, with wholesale contracts totaling roughly $2 million. She informed me, "But as we all know, starting a fashion business is tough, and starting a fashion business based on artisan handwork in the US is quite challenging. She gave birth to her second child, a girl, at the same time that her business partner and she finally parted ways in 2006 due to a difference in our perspectives. She made the decision to reinvent herself and rename her company Alabama Chanin. "Identical individuals. "New name," she murmured. And nothing more about New York. Not alone, Chanin was prepared to fully embrace "the nurturing benefits of a small town," as her friend John Paul White puts it. The internet made telecommuting more commonplace.

Additionally, small businesses could now afford to open online stores thanks to the development of simpler, less expensive point-of-sale software as well as apps for smartphones and tablets. Before those technological developments, a hyperlocal movement didn't seem feasible. Locations such as Florence were too far, too estranged from the New York-London-Paris-Milan retail and design grid. Small villages have become fashion hotspots thanks to the same technology that made globalisation easier for giants like Zara and

H&M to make and sell so much. The power structure was upended and the status quo disrupted. Chanin made contact with Terry Wylie, the previous owner of Tee Jays, who was still the owner of Building 14, and worked out a deal to take over 20,000 square feet of the 160,000 square foot structure.

She moved into the red brick house and packed up operations. Her new apartment felt like a throwback to the early nineties. She recalled, "There was still a pay phone on the wall." Since then, she has expanded to 40,000 square feet, double the initial amount. Divided by corrugated metal and plywood walls, her studio is furnished with worktables, twelve sewing machines, and a library with hundreds of books on sewing, American craft, and southern cookery. She frequently draws inspiration from her vast collection of jerseys and embroidery designs that she has created over the years. She handed me some needlework swatches and said, "I've always imagined that one day we'd go to Paris with these and say, 'These are the things we can do.'" Send us your creative work!She purchases her textiles from Signet Mills in Spartanburg, South Carolina; jersey made of organic Texas cotton is her go-to fabric. For her indigo pieces, she collaborates with a nearby artisan dyer. Her commitment to using organic materials helped her win the 2013 CFDA/Lexus Eco-Fashion Challenge, a recognition and development award for sustainable fashion. The designs are created by Chanin, and her helpers carry them out.

Sue Hanback, a sixty-eight-year-old former garment employee, was her sample sewer when I visited. Chanin remarked, "She basically came out of retirement to help us." Even though Hanback has since retired once more, he still helps out when needed. "We could not have done it without Sue." Chanin employs stencils, "a universal form of pattern transfer," which was initially devised by the Chinese in AD 100, in place of printing on her fabrics, like Mary Katrantzou does. There are currently roughly seven hundred, some geometric and others flowery. Created using a range of materials, such as pasteboard and incredibly durable Mylar that is reusable for hundreds of uses, the designs are applied to the fabric using an airbrush gun. Following the cutting and stencilling of the fabric, as well as the selection of the embroidery supplies and tools, the team puts everything together into what Chanin refers to as a "kit." When a client places an online order, Chanin's independent seamstresses—roughly two dozen in total—bid for the work. All of them are self-employed independent contractors who set their own hours, locations, and clients. They also factor in additional expenses like supplies, utilities, insurance, and other benefits when submitting their bids. According to her explanation, the project is awarded "on timeliness or quality of work." After driving to Building 14, the contracted sewer picks up the kit, stitches it in a day or two, numbers and signs the completed item, and returns it to Alabama Chanin Headquarters so that it may be packaged and shipped to the client.

The retail price of a hand-sewn double-layer organic cotton jersey dress is approximately $800, while the hand-sewn organic cotton coats by Chanin cost nearly $4,000. Depending on the intricacy of the job, her sewers receive a minimum of 25 to 50 percent of the total retail price. "Your things are so expensive!," my friends observed to me as I was having supper with them last night.And I'm like, 'Yeah, screw it, they are. Since I compensate my employees fairly, I don't drive a Mercedes. My vehicle is a Prius. I lead a very simple life." Chanin makes every effort to stay away from labour disputes that have long plagued the south's garment sector. Many people enquire, "How do you know it's not child labour?" Well, we've known Miss Betty for sixteen years now," she informed me. Her age is eighty-six years.

She works only on one type of project. Because of this, we have a rule requiring all of our sewers to reside within an hour and a half of us; you must pick up and drop off your work personally. She doesn't have any children at her house, and she crochets snap covers. It's quite obvious that someone isn't doing it themselves if they come in and take fifty kits every week. It's just that the connection is more intimate. And there are just women involved.I enquired. She declared, "It's all women." Machine-made clothing was introduced by Chanin in 2013. It is manufactured at Bldg. 14 and costs anything from $59 to $1,000, "depending on intricacies," according to Chanin. It was less than the portion of her business she had hoped for. "Finding sewers who can run the machines to a quality standard limits our production capacity," the spokesperson stated. She has teamed up with NEST, a non profit organisation based in New York that helps artisan fashion communities all around the world, to train more machinists.

Additionally, Chanin offers DIY kits for those who like to sew their own clothing. The kits range in price from $150 for a T-shirt to $550 for a wrap dress. She opened the shop and the café about the same time. Six days a week, the café serves lunch in long rows of white-painted wood tables paired with mismatched farm chairs. The shop, an open area that flows into the café, offers a selection of Chanin clothing along with covetable southern artisanal homewares. The chalkboard behind the bar said, "Welcome friends," on the day I went. A small portion of China's current business is wholesale to establishments she enjoys or that are owned by friends, like the Smilow Mathiesen gallery in Santa Fe and the Blackberry Farm hotel in the Tennessee Smoky Mountains. However, the bulk of her sales are made-to-order items that are sold online, typically with a three- to six-week delivery window. Two years later, e-commerce accounted for eighty percent of her business, up from sixty percent when I visited her in 2016.

About 120 clothes are produced every day using Chanin's "lean method of manufacturing," as she refers to it; this is a drop in the ocean compared to the 35 million clothes the Tee Jays factory produced annually during its peak before NAFTA. She created a ten-year plan in 2013 with the objective of hitting $10 million in sales by 2023. She acknowledged that adopting a more moral business model hasn't been "the most lucrative" way to run her company, but with $3 million in revenue in 2018, she added, "We are spot-on for our annual goals." Along the road, she encountered numerous Cassandras who informed her that maintaining a flawless domestic supply chain was unattainable. She remarked, "But even though it wasn't the easiest thing to do, we've stuck to our standards."

Yes, there are moments when working in northwest Alabama makes "us miss the deeper connection to the industry and the heartbeat of what's happening in design in America," but she acknowledged that they have succeeded. However, those melancholy moments of longing are outweighed by the benefits of being "hyperlocal," as she puts it. Because of "our overhead and expenses being so low, it's not as frightening" when the "difficult times come around," which they do. "I own everything on my own; I have no partners. The bank is not owed by us. We don't take out loans to make the collection. We provide youth with quality training and investment. We are really devoted to our community. I've been able to raise my kids, lead a fulfilling creative life, and accomplish worthwhile and significant work. I'm happy with where I am now and the work we have produced. And like CHANIN, Billy Reid had to stumble before realising that small-town slow fashion was the way to go.

However, he's glad to have been involved in bringing something back to his community and contributing to its future. Reid, a second-generation clothes vendor, was born in 1964 and raised in Amite City, a Louisiana bayou backwater located one and a half hours northwest of New Orleans. His mother, T.J. In the old house of his grandmother, Reid operated a clothes business. "I always compare it to Steel Magnolias in a store," Reid said to me when I was in Florence. Reid had higher goals, and for a while he achieved them. "My mother didn't care if customers shopped; they might just come to talk and gossip," Reid said. He started Dallas-based William Reid, a wholesale-focused record company, in 1998. He had thirty-five accounts in two seasons, including Saks Fifth Avenue. He relocated the business to New York in 2000, establishing itself in a warehouse on Manhattan's Twenty-Eighth Street, which runs between Tenth and Eleventh Avenues.

Vogue featured him and he dressed stars like Gwyneth Paltrow and Matthew McConaughey. He received the Perry Ellis Award for Emerging Talent in June 2001, the first of his four Council of Fashion Designers of America (CFDA) nominations. On September 10, 2001, he held his Spring-Summer 2002 fashion presentation at his offices. "Amazing show," he remembered. However, nobody got an opportunity to peruse the reviews or purchase the clothing. The American economy, including Reid's new venture, was severely damaged by the terrorist attack that occurred the following morning. Retailers cancelled orders and appointments, and the $10 million guarantee from his new financial backer was withdrawn. His only option was to give up six months later. "Everything was lost," he informed me. With two tiny children and two large dogs in tow, he and his wife, Jeanne, withdrew to Florence, where they took up residence at her parents' home. His attempt to reestablish his company in New York was unsuccessful. His associates and pals, Katy and K.P.

Another thought that McNeill had was to develop a lifestyle brand that celebrated Reid's southern heritage. They created and presented to him a business proposal. He thought it was good, and in 2004 he and K.P. founded Billy Reid, a Florence-based company. Billy serves as creative director, Katy as chief merchandising officer, and me as chief executive. "We stood out from the start because we were in Florence," K.P. informed me in 2016 as we strolled around the business's offices, located in a classy early-20th-century building on the town's main street, above Reid's shop. It would be far more difficult if Billy were just another designer in New York.

The biggest distinction between the now-defunct William Reid and the constantly expanding Billy Reid is that the 2.0 version is primarily direct-to-consumer, whether through his own boutiques or online. If we were there, I don't think we could run successfully. From the beginning, wholesale was restricted and has been smaller every year. The breakdown was as follows when I saw Reid in 2016: 40% was wholesale, with half going to department shops and the other half to specialised boutiques like Oak Hall in Memphis and Shaia's in Birmingham; 60% was direct-to-consumer, of which 15% was e-commerce. "Traditional retailers, they have experience and expertise," K.P. stated. Not just Billy Reid is moving away from department store chains. Retail giants including Macy's, Lord & Taylor, and Neiman Marcus in the US, as well as John Lewis and House of Fraser in the UK, have recorded plummeting sales and earnings in recent years, and several of them have shuttered their doors, leaving suburban malls without anchor stores.

McNeill informed me that "department stores will be gone in the next three to five years," repeating a complaint I've heard from a lot of people in the fashion industry. "The way business is conducted has fundamentally changed. The future lies in direct-to-consumer sales. As with all corporate decisions, this one has been fueled by profit margins and efficiency. Reid used to only sell wholesale, so each season he had to create and produce 250–300 looks to show retailers during Fashion Week. Of those, buyers would choose about a third—usually the most basic and marketable, like black pants and white shirts—and Reid would pocket between 30 and 40 percent of the retail price. The leftover samples were discarded. Reid creates as he pleases, offers more daring items, avoids redundancy, controls distribution, and keeps 60 to 70 percent of the money customers pay, which he reinvests back into the business to make higher-quality clothing. Reid's company is vertically run, meaning he has a hand in every aspect, from design to retail. Billy Reid was profitable three years following its launch. Sales for the brand totaled $25 million annually by 2017. According to McNeill, "I believe those who are fully vertical—who offer an entire culture and vision—will succeed in the US today." "You are not merely stitching a blouse for an individual who is undercutting you financially. That isn't the case. You can actually pay a little bit extra.

Large corporations tend to view outsourcing as a third-party cut-and-sew process. However, there is a way to use this new model—this new approach—to generate more money over the long run. "This is the holy grail: place the order, and the garment will be made and shipped in twenty-four hours," he said. I answered, "Like fast fashion." "In a good manner," he conceded. There are some things that are just not possible. It is not possible to wash and embroider a pair of jeans in a single day. However, if the cloth is ready, the item is manufactured and sent out. There isn't a wholesale store. Real estate costs none. We removed all obstacles, including inventory risk and expense, according to Reid. "If you do it right and do it real, you can do it from anywhere." * IN 2011, K.P. During harvest season, McNeill was passing by some nearby cotton fields when he had an idea: why not "move from seed to completed product in the same community?

"Vertical integration at its best. Why not hold the event in Florence? There was, after all, a long-standing textile heritage in the area, the cost would be affordable, and there was still the local know-how to tackle the project, the equipment to turn the soil, and, because of Reid and Chanin, a plethora of young creative talent enthusiastic about all things Americana and sustainable. Reid and Chanin embraced McNeill's concept when he presented it to them. Reid and Chanin intended to go back to that business model, but with a modern twist: it would be organic. Prior to NAFTA, Chanin said, the local textile and garment industries "were growing the cotton; they were ginning the cotton; they were processing it." They went "straight from field to form." They contacted the Texas Organic Cotton Marketing Cooperative for seed and the Sustainable Cotton Project in Winters, California, for growing advice. Today, genetically modified cotton makes up 99 percent of the crop.

According to Chanin, "we discovered that there is a shortage of [organic] cotton seeds on the planet." "We spent months looking for this. They eventually gathered enough to sow their first crop, and it was truly terrifying. There were sceptics. All of the farmers were saying, "This is not going to happen," as Chanin observed. "So many people were betting against us, saying that you can't grow cotton unless you use pesticides. You can't grow cotton here." Bugs are going to consume it. It will vanish. "Good luck, ha ha," remarked Lisa Lentz, who jointly owned the project's farmland with her husband, Jimmy Lentz. "We had a drought, and this little cottonfield was planted just like our grandpas would have." We didn't use any water. We took no action," Chanin remarked. "We manually pulled weeds as they appeared, but in certain areas the weeds simply took over. "People drove from all over," she told me, "and the cotton still grew and thrived." Some people even flew in from San Francisco for the harvest in the spring of 2012. We also held a cotton-picking celebration.

Half a hectare. Six hundred pounds. Three hundred individuals. They were laughing and singing together. The cotton was packaged and delivered to Scruggs & Vaden, a nearby gin, for the purpose of eliminating the seeds. After that, it was sent to the fifty-year-old Hill Spinning Mill in North Carolina, where it was spun into thread. In order to prevent traditional cotton's chemicals from contaminating the organic cotton, the mill's machinery was thoroughly cleaned before the organic cotton was processed. The mill owner claimed that he had never seen hand-picked cotton that was immaculate. To produce socks, Gina Locklear of the Little River Sock Mill in Fort Payne, Alabama, received some of the thread. Referred to as the Sock Queen of Alabama, Locklear is a mill owner of the second generation. In 1991, Gina and her sister Emily's parents, Terry and Regina, created a plant called Emi-G, where they produced white sport socks for Russell Athletic. With a population of 14,000, Fort Payne was dubbed "the Sock Capital of the World" in the past because one in every eight pairs produced worldwide came from its more than 150 manufacturers.

After the Central American Free Trade Agreement (CAFTA) was implemented, Honduras gained the upper hand in business dealings with Fort Payne. Though they received very few commands, the Locklears held fast. They were aware that they would never reopen if they closed. "All we would do is come here and sit," Terry Locklear stated. Gina took the lead in 2008, when she was twenty-eight years old. She was a fervent environmentalist who wished to merge her interests in sustainability and socks. She informed me that Zkano, which means "za-ka-no" in Alabama Native American, "loosely translates as a state of being good," and that she created a line of organic cotton socks at the family mill. Bold colours and jazzy graphic designs are used. Her second line, Little River Sock Mill, an Americana-inspired collection with softer hues, more subdued patterns, and retro flower themes, debuted in 2013. Everything was selling nicely, and the plant was back up and running.

Locklear had already worked on a few projects with Reid and Chanin. Thus, when Chanin extended her hand to grab this one, "Oh, I was thrilled!"Before I started making socks, I have always admired Natalie and Billy because of the positive light they were shining on our communities and our state," Locklear told me. Furthermore, cotton was now being grown in our state as well. That was amazing. Locklear made a few hundred pairs of socks in simple shapes with no designs or dyes. She remembered, "Our technicians were really impressed—they said it ran really well." The remaining Chanin-Reid cotton was woven into cloth by Green Textile (now Signet Mills) in Spartanburg, South Carolina (about seven hundred yards' worth), and it was shipped back to Florence to be made into garments. "I remember them saying: 'Great cotton.'" "We completed the cotton cycle in approximately a year," Chanin stated. She handed me one of the V-neck T-shirts and said, "We proved it could be done." It's one of the most well-crafted and comfy shirts I've ever had, made of a soft, dense vanilla jersey with a sturdy seam. * DURING 2018 K.P. and Katy McNeill departed from Billy Reid and Florence in pursuit of a new journey two hours northward in Nashville. They took over Imogene + Willie, which is pronounced "Eye-muh-gene and Willie."

This local casual wear brand is favoured by fashion elites for its vintage, form-fitting jeans, which were sewn in the shop's atelier in the beginning. In terms of the slow fashion trend, Imogene + Willie is a cautionary tale since it expanded so quickly. Its founders lost their way, shifted operations to Los Angeles, and abandoned their initial hyperlocal goal in favour of something larger and more industrial. Less than ten years after its inception, the brand was on the edge of disappearance until the McNeills restored it to its original location—a renovated 1950s filling station in Nashville's hip 12 South area.

Following the slow-fashion, direct-to-consumer approach, they eliminated wholesale and exclusively sold their products online or in their single store. Sales were approaching $3 million by the end of their first year (2018), and they planned to reach $10 million in five years. Their motto is, "Take small steps, don't grow for the sake of growing," K.P. stated. They eventually want to produce in the greater Nashville area, even if a large portion of the line is still made in Los Angeles. Nashville has long been known as America's Music City, and he stated that keeping manufacturing close will allow them "to make sure everything we do we can be proud of." On the other hand, after New York and Los Angeles, it is the third-biggest fashion district in the country. A significant portion of the output involves government contracts, mostly for military uniforms because it is illegal by federal legislation to outsource such work. Naturally, the local entertainment industry has long had a sizable costume business; just consider the extravagantly adorned outfits made popular by celebrities like Elvis Presley, Dolly Parton, and Jack White.

But during the past ten years, straight-up fashion has emerged as a significant third market. Similar to Florence, the main attraction of Nashville is its affordability; living and working expenses are far lower in Nashville than they are in New York or Los Angeles. Nashville is one of the fastest-growing cities in the country, with over 100 new residents relocating there every day—double the national rate. This is an often-cited statistic. A readily accessible international airport, the absence of a state income tax, an abundance of lakes and rivers (water is a requirement in the creation of clothing), and the city's creative culture are further alluring draws for clothing enterprises. According to a 2017 analysis by the Nashville Fashion Alliance (NFA), the fashion industry generated $5.9 billion in sales and 16,200 employment in the region. By 2025, the NFA projected that these statistics would rise to $9.5 billion and 25,000 jobs, respectively.

One hundred plus enterprises, or more than half of them, had been founded in the previous five years. Furthermore, Nashville Fashion Week, a non-profit organisation, presents a series of runway events, panel talks, and exciting parties every spring. Nashville has quickly emerged as a significant player in the US clothing market. Similar to Imogene + Willie, the majority of Nashville-based fashion labels focus on the town's staple wardrobe, which includes selvedge jeans, cotton T-shirts, and chambray shirts. (Nashville is not a good city.) However, there are several innovative designers with large followings. For instance, in 2014 Savannah Yarborough, the former head of menswear at Billy Reid, launched her own custom leather jacket company, Savas.

Additionally, Ceri Hoover is well-known for her handmade shoes and purses. And there's Elizabeth Pape, the creator and designer of the highly regarded Elizabeth Suzann fashion brand. Pape is a rising figure in Nashville fashion. Her first and middle names, Elizabeth Suzann, were created by the self-taught seamstress in her spare bedroom in 2013. The company had grown to $3 million in revenue annually when I met her in 2016 at the early age of twenty-six. It employed eighteen people in ten thousand square feet in an industrial park on the outskirts of town. She wears basic shifts, slouchy slacks, and soft jackets made of cotton, silk, linen, and neutral-toned wool that are all responsibly and, if possible, domestically sourced. Her prices in 2018 ranged from $265 for a canvas coat to $125 for a sleeveless linen crop top.

Additionally, all items are built to order and delivered within two to three weeks. Pape informed me in her showroom that "we don't have an inventory." "No leftovers." Just like at Chanin, every seamstress completes the garment, even down to sewing on the label. Pape has embraced the fast-fashion approach for the mix, showcasing a signature line of timeless pieces interspersed with fresh designs on a regular basis. Although she sells best in New York and Los Angeles, she is happy to not be based in either city since that way, she added, regular customers "come back to us." She remarked, "It's nice to feel a little bit independent and separate." The main challenge Pape has seen in Nashville is the dearth of skilled personnel. "It helps me to not feel overwhelmed and intimidated and just part of this big machine," he says. Twenty-five years ago, NAFTA eliminated the labour force used in the garment industry; people who lost their jobs have either retired, found other employment, or passed away. Home economics classes vanished at the same period.

Pape trained every member of her team herself, remarking that "young people aren't really interested in sewing" these days. In Nashville's developing apparel business, the lack of needleworkers is "one of the biggest challenges," according to Van Tucker, the former head of the Nashville Fashion Alliance. The NFA and Catholic Charities of Tennessee have set up a school to educate refugees how to sew in order to make up for the shortfall. Sewing jobs remain a starting point for immigrants chasing the American dream, just as they were in New York a century ago. The whole production team at Nashville's Omega Apparel, which had made it through the NAFTA exodus by landing military contracts and was branching out into streetwear like T-shirts and hoodies when I visited in 2016, was made up of immigrants and refugees employed through the Catholic Charities program.

The majority were from politically volatile regions like Sudan, Syria, Iran, and Myanmar. A number of the women were Muslim and wore headscarves in the customary manner. A bell rang, indicating noon.

"We communicate through Google Translate," one of the managers told me, "but they are learning English." The smells of several world cuisines flooded the room as the sewers took a seat at a big table near their work area and opened their lunch boxes. Entrepreneur David Perry plans to establish a new knitwear plant in Nashville at the beginning of 2020. Perry, a transplant from Britain in his early fifties, has been making high-end knits and sportswear in Los Angeles since 2007. In order to follow his wife, Leigh, who is from Louisville, Kentucky and sings with the Americana duo Watson Twins, he moved to Nashville. Starting ex novo allowed Perry the opportunity to construct the manufacturing centre of his dreams; at the time he moved, "the living wage here [was] less than minimum wage in California." Nashville has since won him over on both a personal and business level.

He thinks it will be "Tennessee's first fully transparent, fully sustainable factory," powered by solar energy and manned by people paid several dollars an hour above the federal minimum wage. Initially, he will bring in some of his workers from L.A. He stated, "They are great speed sewers, and the fastest driver is essential if you're going to start a race team." After assisting them in a smooth transition to the neighbourhood, he intends to employ local workers, including his best L.A. group. A design centre, a fabric showroom, sourcing consultants—"everything except dyeing"—will also be housed at the factory, he added. "You can come here and we will assist you from beginning to end if you are a New York brand looking to produce in the United States.

Instead of being two thousand miles away in L.A. or elsewhere, production will be there at your doorstep. Billy Reid and Imogene + Willie have both indicated interest in sourcing there. The L.A. The garment manufacturing sector was founded, according to Perry, on an unworkable business model that mostly relied on exploiting workers who were either undocumented or underpaid. "We don't have a broken industry to fix" in Nashville. We have the chance to establish an industry properly. I want customers to go in and say, "This is fantastic." I will tell them, "This is my price, this is the right way to do it, and we will give you the ability to proudly support American jobs and ethically practise." "This is the ideal way to do manufacturing," said Tower Mill. © 2015 Alamy Stock Photo / Chris Bull.

Conclusion

My visits to Florence and Nashville demonstrated to me the viability, profitability, common sense, and envy of slow fashion on a moderate scale—that is, $5 to $10 million in income annually. Could their deliberate, hyperlocal approach to business, however, be extended from cut-and-sew workshops to factories with assembly lines and hundreds or thousands of workers? Is it possible to rekindle domestic manufacturing in wealthy economies using this approach? I was going to learn it at Cottonopolis, of all places. I visited Stalybridge, a mill town that Friedrich Engels described as "repulsive" and "consumed by shocking filth" in 1845. Tameside, the borough that contains Stalybridge, is full of abandoned Victorian-era mills that have been converted into apartments, offices, supermarkets, and even gyms. I travelled there on a mouse-grey November morning in 2016, east of Manchester, England.

Tameside is now tidy. It is now a middle-class suburban area. It has also resurrected as a centre for cotton milling: Tower Mill, a redbrick monolith with a commanding smokestack, was producing Gossypium for a new business called English Fine Cottons, over 70 years after it had stopped operations. I was greeted by Tracy Hawkins, the commercial director. A robust blonde in her early fifties with extensive experience in the British fashion world, she acknowledged that she was exhausted. "We built a modern mill from scratch" in six months, she said. I happened to visit English Fine Cottons on their second full day of operation, and I saw the first large-scale cotton spinning production in the UK in over thirty years, but it's done, and it's working.

English Fine Cottons was not a priority at first. The historic Tame Valley Mill in Tameside is owned by Manchester-born and bred entrepreneurs Brendan McCormack and Steve Shaughnessy, who spin the technical yarn for Kevlar. Over the years, they also got requests to process cotton; but, they consistently declined, stating that it wasn't their business, even though the UK garment industry's textile business had long since perished. Industrial tech textiles are still in demand and simpler to scale in developed nations. Subsequently, Tower Mill, situated right across Tame Valley Mill's street, was listed for sale in 2014. The renowned Victorian architect Edward Potts created the design for this four-story mill, which housed 44,000 spindles at its height when it was constructed in 1885. Tower Mill has been home to a number of enterprises since it closed in 1955. It was also used as a set for the BBC television series Making Out in the early 1990s.

In the early 2000s, there was discussion about turning Tower Mill into opulent condominiums. The plant was put up for sale at the same time that McCormack and Shaughnessy were thinking about ways to grow their business. They reasoned that perhaps we ought to invest in cotton. However, they were opposed to resurrecting the Dickensian horrors of the old milling paradigm. With a private investment of £2.8 million ($3.65 million) from parent company Culimeta-Saveguard, a £2 million ($2.6 million) loan from the Greater Manchester Combined Authority's investment fund, and a £1 million ($1.3 million) grant from the Textile Growth Programme, the partners bought Tower Mill, restored it, and outfitted it with the newest technology. "We wanted to create a place of excellence, producing well-crafted yarns," Hawkins told me. "Not a museum." After addressing the business plan, Hawkins came to the conclusion that "flexibility" and "quality" were the keys to success. By "spin yarns from the thickest counts to the finest—for weaving, knitwear, socks, anything that's needed," she meant that the mill needed to be able to achieve this.

"Why would we want to reinvent an entire industry by positioning ourselves as the only cotton spinners in Britain and then say, 'Oh, we're not interested unless you want to buy five hundred tons?'""The artisanal way of approaching the business, provenance, heritage, and Britishness," she stated, were the qualities she wished to ensure. They would only purchase the best cotton; they initially gave organic cotton some thought, but discovered that it was scarce and of varying quality. In the end, they settled on the ultrasoft Sea Island strain from Barbados and Supima, a sustainable superfine long-staple grown in the United States. According to Hawkins, Sea Island cotton was once used to make the traditional English shirt. "It was what Ian Fleming claimed James Bond's shirts were made of." The next difficulty was to locate a skilled spinner to run their high-tech equipment. How were we going to find someone capable of constructing and managing a contemporary mill?

Hawkins pondered. Though these were hardly employable abilities in the twenty-first century in Britain, she had heard that Paul Storah, a Yorkshireman with expertise in setting up and managing state-of-the-art cotton mills in South Africa, had returned to his native country. He was hired by her to be the operations manager. "There was a small amount of stardust sprinkled there," she grinned and informed me. The mill is a maze of industrial rooms filled with buzzing machinery and winding passageways. Owners in the pretech era depended on the humid atmosphere of the Manchester area to control the "fly," or flying filaments. These days, the cotton is moved from one processor to the next by a network of massive hydraulic tubes.

The majority of the processors are self-contained and include blowers that separate the fibres, blenders that combine different cotton grades, combers that extract the short filaments, or my personal favourite, the "foreign-particle remover," a large glass box filled with cotton that resembles an enormous movie theatre popcorn maker. Lasers search the hazy mass for stray seeds, leaves, or twigs, and if any are found, an extremely fine air jet shoots the trash out. Everything is managed by lab technicians using PCs in a clean room. Twenty-five to thirty times an hour, the facility's air is replaced. Hawkins explained to me that modern cotton spinning is "all about having clean air," since the cotton is quickly processed through a number of machines until "it has a fantastic lustre, it's light, and it's straight." It was more pure, fluffy, and attractive at every location—exactly how you imagine cotton to be. It is only then spun into a yarn at a startling 15,000 to 20,000 . There's no avoiding the fact that flies emit. But the spinning machines are outfitted with customised vacuum robots, rather than depending on the moist air to tamp it down or, as in the nineteenth century, kids with little brooms to sweep between the spindles.

One of the last remaining traditional dye facilities in Britain, Blackburn Yarn Dyers, is located north of Manchester and receives the ivory yarn to be dyed. Hawkins showed me spools of putty white, blue, and grey finished goods. It was smooth, attractive, and as thin as thread. In order to survive outsourcing, John Spencer (Textiles) Ltd., a sixth-generation weaver in the adjacent town of Burnley, Lancashire, became the sole certified weaver of organic cotton yarns in Britain. They would use this yarn to make socks for the UK mass retailer Marks & Spencer. By 2018, English Fine Cottons was manufacturing its own namesake label fabric through a contracted weaver. Marks & Spencer (men's shirts) and Aquascutum (outerwear) are two of its customers.

At Tower Mill, McCormack and Shaughnessy created over a hundred jobs in spite of all the automation. In its initial year of operation, English Fine Cottons produced 100 tons of yarn; by 2018, that amount had increased to 450 tons. Hawkins told me the mill was operating around-the-clock and that they had to hire extra workers because demand was so great when I last spoke with her in the fall of 2018. The only large-scale cotton mill in Britain at the time was English Fine Cottons. It provided weavers with supplies across the nation; Peter Reed and Burberry purchased its yarn, citing it as "the best bed linen you get in the UK," she boasted. * In recent years, RESHORING—the process of resuming production that was offshored during the post-NAFTA globalisation boom—has gained traction, particularly in the fashion industry. After electrical and transportation equipment, textiles and clothing was the third most offshored industry in the US in 2014.

It grew at the second-fastest rate in 2016, employing 135,000 people and producing 10% of the country's fashion, a remarkable increase from 3% in 2013. The number of jobs in the UK producing clothing increased by 9% between 2011 and 2016, reaching 100,000, with an additional 20,000 jobs predicted to be added by 2020. The reshoring trend of today is not in line with the Panglossian idea of "Make America Great Again," which held that all laid-off workers might return to their previous positions if businesses repatriated the work they had offshored in the 1990s and 2000s. The truth is that during the course of the next 25 years, the majority of those employees "aged out." Furthermore, fashion does not advance while the same stale Arkwright business model is continued. Instead, English Fine Cottons and its associates are engaging in "rightshoring," which is the revival of domestic production using cutting-edge technology and transparency, frequently in factories that have lain idle for a long time.

According to Van Tucker, the former chairman of the Nashville Fashion Alliance, rightshoring "looks different than manufacturing looked in the 1980s." He also told me that innovation will spread swiftly. Social issues are significant, sustainability in particular. It's also tech-driven. Extremely automated," describes the trend as "a reversal" of globalisation as it has been understood by Paul Donovan, global head economist at UBS Wealth Management. He believes that global trade of goods, such as apparel, will "revert to something like the old 'imperial model' of importing raw materials and then processing it close to the consumer." Rightshoring doesn't mean mills must source everything nearby—cotton won't be grown in the UK for English Fine Cottons. Instead, it means that we can produce efficiently, locally. Trade wars today are fighting battles from the past.

However, it does entail production in close proximity to the final customer, as in the case of English Fine Cottons spinning yarn for Marks & Spencer socks distributed all throughout Great Britain, or designers procuring locally produced fabrics, as in the case of Natalie Chanin purchasing jerseys woven in the Carolinas.

Contrary to popular belief, technology might eventually make the textile and clothing industries more ethical and humane. Clothes don't have to be manufactured with antiquated equipment by underpaid, maltreated labourers. They can be made in calm, spotless factory floors run by assistants with technical training, in vertically linked communities. It can also occur in places where the manufacturing industry has long abandoned. It's possible that you know those assistants. Otherwise, the plant might be right across the street. Even though automation won't produce thousands of manufacturing jobs, the ones that do will be well-paying, safe, and of high quality—a hundred here, a hundred there. As unlikely as it may seem, technology will introduce people into the supply chain.

The textile and clothing industry in North Carolina was so revitalised by rightshoring that, by 2017, 42,000 people were working in 700 factories—many of which are as sophisticated as those of English Fine Cottons. For the majority of the 20th century,

Parkdale Mills in South Carolina was one of the largest spinning houses in the United States. To manufacture 2.5 million pounds of yarn a week in 1980, the Gaffney-based company would have needed 2,000 workers. The town's mill was put on hold when Parkdale relocated its operations to mainland China following the 2005 WTO-China agreement. 2010 saw the reopening of Parkdale in South Carolina, featuring cutting edge equipment operated by operators from clean rooms with an eye toward the spinning floor. Anderson Warlick, CEO of Parkdale, stated, "We knew in order to survive we'd have to take technology as far as we could." A week, 140 workers can now generate 2.5 million pounds of yarn. Even while it's not the 2,000 jobs from before, it's still 140 jobs over zero. Such success has the potential to spread, with new companies starting other new companies, and so on, until there is a true boom and once-depressed communities become vital once more.

China is one of the countries that contributes financially. The Zhejiang-based Keer Group established a $218 million, 165-acre "textile campus" in Lancaster County, South Carolina, in 2015—creating jobs for over 500 people—becoming its first factory outside of its home province. It is hyper computerised, just like Tower Mill. Naturally, Keer Group's main driving force was financial: milling had become less economical in China due to growing labour and energy expenses. Furthermore, as McCormack and Shaughnessy discovered, it is far simpler to equip a vacant plant with new technology than it is to modernise an existing one. There are no job losses, no employee layoffs, and no current machinery being junked. Zhu Shan Qing, chairman of Keer Group, listed South Carolina's "proximity to cotton producers, and access to the port" as further draws. Furthermore, as McCormack and Shaughnessy found, there are "incentives' ' to rightshore; in Keer's instance, they included tax credits, revenue bonds, and infrastructure subsidies totaling around $20 million. The Carolinas are now home to dozens of high-tech textile mills owned by Chinese nationals, a reality that has some residents gasping for air.

At the time, Keith Tunnell, the president of Lancaster County Economic Development Corporation, admitted, "I never thought the Chinese would be the ones bringing textile jobs back." * In New York City, the challenge has been to support the remaining manufacturing rather than just rightshore it. There have been more successful attempts than unsuccessful ones. The borough president of Brooklyn first announced plans to open a fashion "incubator" at Bush Terminal in Sunset Park back in 1997, but the plans were shelved indefinitely. The Fashion Industry Modernization Centre was established in 1998 by the management-labour Garment Industry Development Corp., but it ultimately failed. West Thirty-Fifth Street-based designer Nanette Lepore spearheaded "Save the Garment Center" protests and pushed Washington legislators for help.

Not much was going to happen. It turns out that the most successful move has been the devotion of talented New Yorkers like Zero + Maria Cornejo (pronounced "Cor-nay-ho"). When the British-educated designer, who was born in Chile, worked in Paris in the late 1980s for the UK mass fashion brand Jigsaw, she witnessed firsthand what she refers to as "the false economy." They would send her to Hong Kong in business class and house her at the five-star Mandarin Oriental Hotel. After that, they would "nickel and dime" the clients she was scheduled to see. As we sat in her book-filled Bleecker Street office, she told me, "They'd say, 'Well, we're going to save a dollar on a sweater, but we're going to ship it halfway across the world." Her English accent was tinged with Spanish. It was incomprehensible to me. Production was "a crazy system," wherein clothing designers from the US and Europe would digitally transfer the specifications to an Asian plant to produce samples. But it didn't work that way.

The completed samples would be delivered to corporate headquarters to be inspected and, most of the time, rejected after much back and forth by phone and email. A well-known New York company would place an order for six hundred samples in China, then "cut it down to two hundred," according to her. "Imagine the waste, would you?"Even if it was just a T-shirt, I wanted to have control over every aspect from start to finish—how it was made, who made it, and how it looks," she said. She desired to go rightshore and said, "I wanted to know those people." She relocated to New York in 1996 with her spouse, photographer Mark Borthwick, and leased an old garage on Mott Street. In 1998, they launched a storefront featuring a sewing studio at the rear, selling what she described as "interesting, easy clothes that you could afford to wear." "I wanted it to be just about the product, and not for people to have preconceived notions of what it should look like or who was behind it," the founder stated, explaining why she chose to name the company Zero.

She made $2,500 on her first day of business. "We saw it as encouraging," she subsequently recollected. She changed the name of hers to Zero + Maria Cornejo after discovering that there was already a well-known German fashion brand with the same name. (The plus sign is pronounced as "plus.") Her group was cohesive and diverse. Shanghai-born immigrant Jiang Huang sewn samples. Tonya was from Russia and handled knitwear (he took over that task after learning how to cut patterns). China native Lynn was in charge of the silks. Cornejo remarked, "She introduced me to Mr. Huang." The labels said, MADE AT 225 MOTT STREET, and she sold the clothing out front in her boutique. "And I cut everything." "I recall having a disagreement with a woman once on the cost of my clothing, and I responded by saying, 'You see all those people working in the back? Their residence is in New York. They receive just compensation.

This rent is paid by us. It's not like the clothing that is transported to Timbuktu to be manufactured by child labour." Soon, Barneys called, just like with Natalie Chanin, and before long, Cornejo had a sizable fan base that included Cindy Sherman, Michelle Obama, and Tilda Swinton. She controlled her growth by limiting her purchases to women's clothing and a select few shoes and belts. She declared, "I've never been interested in owning a pair of underpants with my name on them." "The whole idea of obtaining more, more, more, more, just for the sake of getting more doesn't appeal to me. Growth doesn't always mean getting bigger and bigger. No, it's about setting up the proper conditions and carrying out the necessary tasks. Fine-tuning." In 2008, it was time to go; her shop-atelier had grown into a full-fledged corporation and her rent at the 1,800-square-foot Mott Street premises had quadrupled in 10 years. She saw a For Rent sign on a turn-of-the-century building with windows on three sides while driving down Bleecker Street, which is lined with trees and has cobblestones. Perfect, she thought, for her new studio. She took 6,000 square feet more, dividing it between the first floor offices for wholesale, retail, and communications, the basement for storage, and the second floor for design, manufacturing, logistics, and finance. She also took 1,500 square feet on the ground level for her shop.

The second-floor workroom was brightly lit on the sweltering summer day I visited, and it was packed with metal rolling racks holding swatches, paper patterns, muslin samples, and finished clothing. The production office was full of under-thirties, busy bees on desktop computers, who wore headphones. Mr. Huang and his design team were doing fittings for the spring-summer collection across the hall. He was looking over a gorgeous cotton velvet dress, the colour of berry, with an asymmetrical neckline when we walked in. Approximately fifty firms manufacture at least 75% of their output in New York City, including Cornejo, who's ready-to-wear is virtually entirely made there. (She hires specialised knitters in Bolivia to create sweaters, sources some knitwear from China and Peru, and relies on Italian leather workers to construct her shoes.) The majority of her suppliers are located in the Garment District, also known as "Thirty-Sixth Street, Thirty-Eighth Street," according to her. "My people immediately go to the Six and inquire about any drama that occurs at the factory." Cornejo has been producing four collections annually since 2009—two for the runway at New York Fashion Week and two exclusively for showroom appointments.

With eight staff, two storefronts (in New York and Los Angeles), an online store, and wholesale sales, she generates approximately $10 million in revenue annually—a figure that Chanin is aiming for. It is decent for a one-woman, privately held business, but it pales in comparison to the $5 to $10 billion that the mega-brands like Dior, Gucci, Chanel, and Louis Vuitton bring in each year. "Midtown Manhattan is the centre of fashion in New York for a reason," the speaker stated. "It's amazing to be able to leave your office and visit your client." * THAT MAY NOT LAST Eternally, at least not if Andrew Rosen, the CEO of Theory and a third-generation fashion designer until recently, has his way. Rosen has been leading the effort for the past few years to move the Garment District to Brooklyn's Sunset Park. There are currently a few stand-alone centres in the municipality. Located in what was once Storehouse No. 2 of the US Navy Fleet Supply Base, Manufacture New York is a fashion incubator formed in 2012 by Bob Bland, a former design assistant for Ralph Lauren.

The Brooklyn Fashion + Design Accelerator is located at Pratt Institute. Located within a collection of renovated textile buildings, the Greenpoint Manufacturing and Design Center is another option. Members of Brooklyn's maker community have visited all three. Mayor Bill de Blasio pledged to construct a Made in New York campus in Brooklyn's Bush Terminal during his State of the City speech at the Apollo Theater in February 2017—exactly like the borough president had unveiled two decades prior. On this occasion, though, the city committed $136 million to the project, which also included facilities for producing movies and television shows. The anticipated opening year is 2020. De Blasio declared, "You're going to see this whole area come alive." There were 1,568 clothing manufacturers in New York City in 2017, with over 25% of them located in or near the Garment District. Furthermore, not everyone is eager to cross the East River. Even many outside the fashion business were concerned when designer Yeohlee Teng expressed concerns at a symposium on the topic that spring, saying, "We look at the district as an incubator." Joe Ferrara, president of the New York Garment Center Supplier Association, mocked the proposal and called it "a deportation."

In opposition, Rosen points out that costume designer Steven Epstein says that if Bette Midler tears the train of her dress because the understudy chorus boy steps on it, the wardrobe supervisor can go to the garment centre, buy the fabric, get it back to the theatre, and get that train recut and stitched before the show even begins. In 2017, he told me in his all-white, west-facing corner office at Theory's headquarters on Gansevoort Street in the Meatpacking District, "I've been a big proponent of trying to reimagine what the Garment Center should look like twenty years from now, not what it looked like twenty years ago." He was a robust man in his early sixties, standing six feet tall, and eating a dish of sashimi off a tray at his desk while he talked. He pressed his chopsticks into the air to emphasise key points. "Many people are scared of [the Brooklyn idea] because they believe no one will go there," according to Chopsticks, including workers, clients, and manufacturers. Chopsticks, though. "People will want to work there, and it'll be a thriving modern industry if we create a new vibrant community with state-of-the-art space and state-of-the-art equipment." Initially, "everything" for Theory was created in New York City. "I could accomplish everything here, so there was no need to travel overseas," he remarked as he continued to enjoy his Japanese meal. He brought up Liz Claiborne's groundbreaking work and said, "But as business diversified globally, there were a lot of advantages to manufacturing overseas price-wise."

He claimed that "they were the first" and that "they changed the game." Because they understood how to manufacture overseas, they were able to grow their business into a multimillion dollar enterprise. Currently, he stated, roughly 25% of Theory's runs—which include "jackets, pants, and tailored things"—are made in New York. The remainder? "All over. China. Vietnam. The company's elegant Design Center, a minifactory a block away on Gansevoort Street, is where samples are created, produced, fitted, and shrink-tested for Theory and Helmut Lang, another brand under the Link Theory group that Rosen managed. The Design Center was established in 2016 and is equipped with the most recent technology, including laser-guided pattern cutting for increased precision and reduced waste, and bonding machines, a system that binds seams rather than sews them.

Once an idea is approved, it's delivered to a Midtown manufacturer or a foreign manufacturer to be made commercially. Though Theory's hybrid model isn't fully rightshored, it is closer to it than rivals who manufacture everything—including samples—offshore. Would Rosen ever return to New York with that offshored work? He remarked, "It's possible if it gets moved and centralised in one place." It makes sense for small US-based companies with yearly sales of $10 million or less to produce domestically. "You can keep your eyes on it, and it's quicker," he remarked. "Making in New York has many benefits, thus I strongly advise young start-ups to do so and to source at least 75% of their goods from here. It's the ideal method for launching a company. He's positive that shifting the Garment District to Sunset Park would make the project much more alluring. "And it's more possible now than even five years ago." The chopsticks pointed east, then west, then south. "One of the problems in New York manufacturing now is that the pattern making is here, the sample making is here, and the cutting is here."

"And the sewing is somewhere else," he remarked, waving his left hand toward Sunset Park. "I think everything can happen out there," he continued, referring to the fashion industry's younger members who all lived in Brooklyn and couldn't afford to be in the city. It might be incredible. It would be possible to have showrooms, manufacturing, and design. "Like a fashion city," I said. Yes, he answered. * DIRECTLY BEHIND MARIA Cornejo's headquarters, on Bond Street, is a boutique selling a more affordable, West Coast version of her hyperlocal, environmentally conscious apparel. He pointed the chopsticks at me. Yael Aflalo, a former model who grew up in Beverly Hills, launched the company Reformation in 2009. Reformation is environmentally friendly. It's open and visible. positioned correctly. Aflalo, however, has far greater goals than Cornejo does.

She does not believe that being "a sustainable fast fashion brand" is an oxymoron. "Quickly has no bearing on environmental impact," she informed me when making clothing. The formula for Aflalo is straightforward: create fun, well-made clothing, such crop tops, A-line minidresses, and capri trousers, in hygienic, above-board factories, mainly in the greater Los Angeles area, and sell it for between $40 and $450.

Additionally, a section was added to the Galeries Lafayette department store in April 2018. They bear well-known labels, and consumers are drawn to brands they are familiar with. They used to seek out brands, but now the other way around is happening. (Chanel had communicated recently.) Like typical merchants, they purchase in bulk, but they only accept two or three sizes of each style and only select a few designs. Delivery, collection, and dry cleaning (mostly by Paris-based eco-cleaner Le Comptoir des Blanchisseurs) are included in the rental price. Monday through Friday, a bicycle courier will deliver the items; if not, buyers can pick them up at Galeries Lafayette or the showroom. Moreover, Panoply will fulfil DHL orders across Europe. On the second anniversary of Panoply's full-time launch, I met Brizay at the Rue Royale store, a converted apartment housed in a stately eighteenth-century structure. She embodies the ideal Parisian: slender, with defined features, unadorned, and a dishwater-blond hairstyle cut short and sassy.

She wore her own black leather leggings by Joseph, a black cashmere sweater by Nicole Farhi, tapestry flats by Charlotte Olympia, and a tuxedo coat by Christopher Kane that she had leased from Panoply that day. Even Friday casual is the end for the French. We sat on mid century chairs with clothes racks all around us. The Parisian tailor Pallas, a favourite of French First Lady Brigitte Macron, was wearing both tuxedos and pantsuits behind me. Diane von Furstenberg wrapped dresses in the corner. A new arrival behind Brizay: Stella McCartney coats, suits, and dresses. One-shot customers include everyone from eighty-year-olds seeking for gowns fit for the grandmother of the bride to teens searching for party outfits. The subscriber base consists of professional women between the ages of 35 and 55. Panoply recorded 5,000 subscribers and roughly 6,000 one-shot buyers in 2018. Sara Dalloul, the head of business and marketing at Panoply, revealed, "It's still hush-hush." Not too, though. With seven or eight patrons every day, the showroom is constantly busy. I thought it would be appropriate to rent my attire because I was attending a seminar at the Centre for Sustainable Fashion in London the next week.

I was taken in hand by thirty-year-old caramel-complexioned Parisienne Bettina Hetoubanabo, a panoply stylist speckled with freckles. I adored her outfit: a black bottle, black pants, white camisole, and mocha dreads that, halfway through, turned gold and were arranged in an ice cream swirl. "Selling is so outdated," she said to me while passing me a navy wool suit by Stella McCartney with a chequered fuchsia windowpane design. "The new perspective is to rent." I never would have picked out the suit on my own, with its boxy jacket and cropped trousers in such a vibrant pattern. Furthermore, I couldn't afford it at the retail price of €1,720. To rent it for €255, though? That was manageable. She stretched a silk camisole by Phillip Lim (€400 retail/€48 rental), so I gave it a go. I'm not really into camis. I was surprised, though, how well the ensemble looked. When Brizay stated that renting clothing gives women more confidence and daring, I knew exactly what she meant. One essay changed my personal style to something far more fashionable.

Dalloul stated, "Our stylists look after our clients from A to Z." "Our stylists will create and send a mood board if a client says, 'I have a bar mitzvah in two weeks. I want something to cover my arms because I don't like to show them.'" In order to rent, a subscriber purchases a pack of credits (one credit costs €69, three cost €159, and five cost €229), which they then distribute as needed, much like tickets at an amusement park. (A larger credit pack will result in a lower rental cost.) It would cost me one credit for the camisole and three credits for the outfit. Unfortunately, the camisole was already rented, but I had the suit all to myself for eight days. The following day it was brought by bike, and I took it with me to London. I ate up compliments during the meeting. I gained additional praise when I replied that I had rented it. How enduring! How cyclical!

Among the €1.7 million ($1.9 million) that Panoply raised in 2016 was from the investment fund Experienced Capital. And when I met them, they were preparing to start a second round, to quadruple that amount. (To put it in context, Blue Pool, the investment group that manages the wealth of Alibaba founders Jack Ma and Joe Tsai, contributed $20 million of the $210 million that Rent the Runway raised by 2018.) Chic by Choice, a British rental provider, was acquired by Panoply in 2017. Along with it came a 350,000-strong database and Clean Cleaners, a sustainable dry cleaning business. Panoply became the top fashion rental firm in Europe as a result of the acquisition. Brizay and Brochard intend to expand much further. Pop-up stores in London. Brizay explained that the partnership with Air France will enable premium customers travelling from Japan to Paris to have rental services available, "so people can travel luggage-free." a "white label," allowing brands to rent directly to customers while Panoply acts as an intermediary in an anonymous manner. (Rent the Runway was considering doing this as well.) Perhaps even an alliance with Rent the Runway to deliver a smooth service on the other side of the Atlantic. like a worldwide network of rentals.

The Circular Economy Roadmap for France was unveiled by Prime Minister Édouard Philippe in the spring of 2018. Among the proposals are laws that would forbid shops and fashion labels from burning or discarding unsold merchandise. Rather, the remainder would need to be given to recyclers or charities (which is good news for Worn Again and Evrnu). Panoply perceives a chance there. Perhaps they will take the leftovers and let them go as well. * A LOT of the participants in Fashionopolis are not entirely aligned. The slow-fashion crowd has a different goal and scale than the rightshorers; high fashion is still about seasons and, as Stella McCartney herself acknowledges, creating new things. That's not the perspective you'll find at businesses that are attempting to repurpose and reengineer current materials. The Sewbots and Alabama Chanin may not have the same objectives, but they both have the potential to contribute to the solution for the atrocities represented by Bangladesh sweatshops. Rent the Runway and Moda have completely distinct business models.

It will require all of these strategies—along with many more—to address the intricate and colossal mess that is currently Fashionopolis and create a better, more equitable fashion environment. Every person this book highlights is resisting a model that is blatantly unworkable in their own unique way. that exalts limitless consumerism, steadily declining costs (whether attained by the theft of another person's work of art or their human rights), and steadily rising profits. That purposefully produces leftovers. That doesn't consider the environmental toll it causes. The producers won't be the only ones to spark the revolution. It is up to us all to step up. Purchase less things. We use several washing methods for our garments. Fix or repurpose them further. Think about how the material they are made of affects them. Think about the chain of production that creates them. Think about the principles of the company that produced and marketed them. We must develop a personal style that benefits the world more than it harms. And for the time being, renting might be the greenest option available.

Although you can update your look at any time, the individual components have a lengthy lifespan. It somewhat sustains the current state of the apparel industry. Indeed, just as all these other movements and technologies have been since Arkwright engaged the first water frame, renting is also susceptible to bastardization. Everything might speed up with faster consumption, including creation, production, and sales floor drops. If we don't feel anything for our garments, will we care about them any less? If they are like speed dates, coming and going from our lives? Do you think renting will ever be the ultimate way to say "I really don't care"? Hopefully not. I hope that we would see our clothing as the full ecology that it is, rather than just something we throw on. I'll be serious about it when I get dressed in the morning, I promise.

Maybe I'll pull on my well-worn, well-crafted Alabama Chanin T-shirt, which is composed of carefully chosen organic cotton, my indigo-dyed Levi's from Stony Creek, which are held up with a Modern Meadow belt, and my sharply designed Stella McCartney jacket, which is made of wool from contented New Zealand sheep. Alternatively, I might rent something sexy to wear out and return it after I'm done. And Stacy Flynn and Cyndi Rhoades will transform everything back into virginal goodness to be woven, dyed, cut, stitched, and worn again when it's all too worn out to wear. I went back to Paris the day following the sustainability conference. And the Panoply courier visited my apartment the following day at noon to retrieve the clothing bag. The outfit has vanished. I felt depressed. It was enjoyable to me.

A great deal. I could see myself purchasing it and using it in my life and wardrobe. Then I made the decision that it should have gone back. Without it, I could survive. There would always be another, after all.